A heart AFTER GOD

A heart AFTER GOD

Erin Wolff
with Rory Wolff

CREATION HOUSE

A Heart After God by Erin Wolff, with Rory Wolff
Published by Creation House
A Charisma Media Company
600 Rinehart Road
Lake Mary, Florida 32746
www.charismamedia.com

Design Director: Bill Johnson
Cover design by Nathan Morgan

Visit the author's website: www.heartaftergodministries.net
Library of Congress Cataloging-in-Publication Data: 2013930881
International Standard Book Number: 978-1-62136-352-1
E-book International Standard Book Number: 978-1-62136-353-8

First edition

13 14 15 16 17 — 987654321
Printed in Canada

DEDICATION AND SPECIAL THANKS

FIRST AND FOREMOST, I want to thank the Lord. The life that Satan had planned for me was a life of pain, heartache, loneliness, bitterness, blindness, and complete and utter emptiness, a life not worth living; but the Lord rescued me and gave me a life of peace, joy, comfort, love, and everything good. I am so thankful to You, Lord, for each and every good and perfect gift that You have so generously poured out upon me.

Second, I would like to thank my dear husband. Thank you, Rory, for your constant love and faithfulness. God blessed me so greatly when He blessed me with you. There is no one in this whole world that I would rather be with. You constantly bless me with who you are and who you are becoming day by day. I love you so much!

I would also like to thank all of my beautiful babies. The Lord has taught me so much patience, love, and joy because of you. Joshua, you are faithful; Hezekiah, you are fascinating; Simeon, you are gentle; Nehemiah, you are witty; Justus, you are determined; Benjamin, you are indomitable; and Hadassah, you are precious. You are all the very best and one of the greatest blessings that I have ever been given. I love you all so much!

And last but definitely not least I want to thank everyone who has helped and encouraged me in the writing of this book.

CONTENTS

INTRODUCTION

In May of 2010, a month and a half after having my fifth baby, the Lord gave me what I thought was a sermon. I wrote out what I believed the Lord told me to say and prayed, asking Him who I should give the sermon to. Within a few days the Lord put it on my heart that it was not a sermon but the first chapter and outline of a book. I felt very humbled and blessed that the Lord would ever give me the privilege to be entrusted with such a service.

Everything the Lord has told me to do in writing this book has brought me further from my comfort zone and has pushed me into a greater relationship and faith in Him. I am a very organized person. A year ago, if I thought the Lord wanted me to write a book I would have sat down with a pencil and pad of paper and started writing down an outline for every chapter, detailing everything. With this book, the Lord told me a name of someone in the Bible, and I looked up the name and read about that person, praying the Lord would give me some sort of revelation. When I got a revelation, the Lord then told me what to write. The whole time I was writing the chapter, I thought, "This can't be right. I must not be hearing correctly, because it doesn't seem to make much sense," but God brought it all together at the end, and I am amazed. I never knew what I was going to write about until the Lord revealed it to me.

This has been a lot of fun for me, watching God work in my life. I am just an ordinary, stay-at-home mom, and I love the Lord with my whole heart and want desperately to know Him more. I want to glorify Him in all of my ways. I try very hard to be a good wife to my husband, submitting to him according to the Word of God, and I strive to be a good mother, teaching my children in the way that they should go, yet trying to hold on to a balanced life at the same time.

It amazes me that God can talk to me while I am changing a poopy diaper, while my children are fighting, the supper is burning, and I've had five bad hours of sleep. What an amazing, tangible God we serve. God is able to be touched and is able to touch us in a very profound way. I desperately want not only the world but the church to know God in an awesome way. I want people to love Him with their whole hearts, having a great desire to persevere through all that this life throws at them, all the while having a firm grasp on God Almighty. I want God's people to be a people without compromise, who trust in the Lord with their whole hearts, trusting Him with everything. I want them to know His furious love yet love Him back for His absolute greatness. I want people to want to give themselves completely to Him, holding nothing back. I want them to fear God, respecting Him for who He is yet knowing Him intimately. The limitlessness of God! I hope and pray that while we look at the lives of some of the greatest men and women of God, we will want to strive for that greatness and along the way fall madly in love with the King of kings and the Lord of lords.

I pray that your life will be a life that is truly lived.

And to truly live your life, you have to trust God and jump into the river. May the adventure be nothing you expected it to be and yet immeasurably better than you ever could have dreamed.

LOTS OF LOVE, ERIN WOLFF

1

JACOB VS. ESAU

Desire God More Than All Things

As the deer pants for streams of water, so my soul pants for you, my God.

—Psalm 42:1

I was watching a show on TV where a man name Darren Wilson was being interviewed. God had told Darren to make a movie about His "furious love." The only thing that God really told Darren was that he must "go into the darkness to show the light." So he decided to go to some of the darkest places on Earth. One of the places he went to was a large witch coven in Salem, Oregon. Darren thought that he and his team were going to go into this coven to start a fight about who was greater, God or Satan, and that there would maybe even be these great shows of power. But instead God had him and the people with him go and love the people. God had them prophesy and speak God's love, grace, and truth over the lives of these lost people.[1]

When I heard this story it really touched me, because I am continually amazed at the love God has. What grace He has not only for the lost but for His own people. To forgive people whose lives are so full of sin and wrongdoing and to lift them out of the bondages that Satan has put them in is truly incredible. It is a love that knows no bounds, a love that pulls people out of darkness and fills them full of light, and a love that breaks the chains of the enemy.

Furious by definition means "very great, intense, and wild." God has spoken some very strong statements in His Word. These statements sound tough and in some ways are tough, but it is only because of His furious, great, intense, wild love for His people that He speaks in such ways. He speaks to us in the way in which Christ was compelled to overturn the tables of the moneychangers and drive out all of the people that were buying and selling in the temple area; that, to me, is intense and wild.

One of those strong statements is found in Malachi 1:2–3. This verse has always been very interesting to me. God says through Malachi, "I have loved Jacob, but Esau I have hated." Wow, what a thing to say. But if you know God, He does not hate people. God is perfect love; He gave up His only Son so that we might live with Him forever. So we know it's not the man that he hated, but what the man represented, what he stood for and his actions.

In the Book of Genesis chapter twenty-five we read the account of Jacob and Esau. Abraham had Isaac, and Isaac married Rebekah.

> Isaac prayed to the Lord on behalf of his wife, because she was childless. The Lord answered his prayer, and his wife Rebekah became pregnant. The babies jostled each other within her,

> and she said, "Why is this happening to me?" So she went to inquire of the LORD. The LORD said to her, "Two nations are in your womb, and two peoples from within you will be separated; one people will be stronger than the other, and the older will serve the younger." When the time came for her to give birth, there were twin boys in her womb. The first to come out was red, and his whole body was like a hairy garment; so they named him Esau. After this, his brother came out, with his hand grasping Esau's heel; so he was named Jacob. Isaac was sixty years old when Rebekah gave birth to them. The boys grew up, and Esau became a skillful hunter, a man of the open country, while Jacob was content to stay at home among the tents. Isaac, who had a taste for wild game, loved Esau, but Rebekah loved Jacob. Once when Jacob was cooking some stew, Esau came in from the open country, famished. He said to Jacob, "Quick, let me have some of that red stew! I'm famished!" (That is why he was also called Edom.) Jacob replied, "First sell me your birthright." "Look, I am about to die," Esau said. "What good is the birthright to me?" But Jacob said, "Swear to me first." So he swore an oath to him, selling his birthright to Jacob. Then Jacob gave Esau some bread and some lentil stew. He ate and drank, and then got up and left. So Esau despised his birthright.
>
> —GENESIS 25:21–34

The first thing you'll notice is that it ends saying, "So Esau despised his birthright." The word *despised* means "to scorn and loathe." *To loathe* means "to feel intense dislike or disgust for." The name *Jacob* actually means "he grasps the heel"; figuratively speaking it means "he deceives." So, it's strange; you have two very different brothers. You have one who despises, loathes, and feels intense dislike for his birthright, and you have the other who was willing to deceive, lie, and cheat in order to get it. Jacob literally coveted after it.

> When Isaac was old and his eyes were so weak that he could no longer see, he called for Esau his older son and said to him, "My son." "Here I am," he answered. Isaac said, "I am now an old man and don't know the day of my death. Now then, get your equipment—your quiver and bow—and go out to the open country to hunt some wild game for me. Prepare me the kind of tasty food I like and bring it to me to eat, so that I may give you my blessing before I die." Now Rebekah was listening as Isaac spoke to his son Esau. When Esau left for the open country to hunt game and bring it back, Rebekah said to her son Jacob, "Look, I overheard your father say to your brother Esau, 'Bring me some game and prepare me some tasty food to eat, so that I may give you my blessing in the presence of the Lord before I die.' Now, my son, listen carefully and do what I tell you: Go out to the flock and bring me two choice young goats, so I can prepare some tasty food for your father, just the way he likes it. Then take it to your father to eat, so that he may give you his blessing before he dies." Jacob said to Rebekah his mother, "But my brother Esau is a hairy man while I have smooth skin. What if my father touches me? I would appear to be tricking him and would bring down a curse on myself rather than a

blessing." His mother said to him, "My son, let the curse fall on me. Just do what I say; go and get them for me." So he went and got them and brought them to his mother, and she prepared some tasty food, just the way his father liked it. Then Rebekah took the best clothes of Esau her older son, which she had in the house, and put them on her younger son Jacob. She also covered his hands and the smooth part of his neck with the goatskins. Then she handed to her son Jacob the tasty food and the bread she had made. He went to his father and said, "My father." "Yes, my son," he answered. "Who is it?" Jacob said to his father, "I am Esau your firstborn. I have done as you told me. Please sit up and eat some of my game, so that you may give me your blessing." Isaac asked his son, "How did you find it so quickly, my son?" "The LORD your God gave me success," he replied. Then Isaac said to Jacob, "Come near so I can touch you, my son, to know whether you really are my son Esau or not." Jacob went close to his father Isaac, who touched him and said, "The voice is the voice of Jacob, but the hands are the hands of Esau." He did not recognize him, for his hands were hairy like those of his brother Esau; so he proceeded to bless him. "Are you really my son Esau?" he asked. "I am," he replied. Then he said, "My son, bring me some of your game to eat, so that I may give you my blessing." Jacob brought it to him and he ate; and he brought some wine and he drank. Then his father Isaac said to him, "Come here, my son, and kiss me." So he went to him and kissed him. When Isaac caught the smell of his clothes, he blessed him and said,

"Ah, the smell of my son is like the smell of a field that the Lord has blessed. May God give you heaven's dew and earth's richness— an abundance of grain and new wine. May nations serve you and peoples bow down to you. Be lord over your brothers, and may the sons of your mother bow down to you. May those who curse you be cursed and those who bless you be blessed." After Isaac finished blessing him, and Jacob had scarcely left his father's presence, his brother Esau came in from hunting. He too prepared some tasty food and brought it to his father. Then he said to him, "My father, please sit up and eat some of my game, so that you may give me your blessing." His father Isaac asked him, "Who are you?" "I am your son," he answered, "your firstborn, Esau." Isaac trembled violently and said, "Who was it, then, that hunted game and brought it to me? I ate it just before you came and I blessed him—and indeed he will be blessed!" When Esau heard his father's words, he burst out with a loud and bitter cry and said to his father, "Bless me—me too, my father!" But he said, "Your brother came deceitfully and took your blessing." Esau said, "Isn't he rightly named Jacob? This is the second time he has taken advantage of me: He took my birthright, and now he's taken my blessing!" Then he asked, "Haven't you reserved any blessing for me?" Isaac answered Esau, "I have made him lord over you and have made all his relatives his servants, and I have sustained him with grain and new wine. So what can I possibly do for you, my son?" Esau said to his father, "Do you have only one blessing, my father? Bless me too, my

> father!" Then Esau wept aloud. His father Isaac answered him, "Your dwelling will be away from the earth's richness, away from the dew of heaven above. You will live by the sword and you will serve your brother. But when you grow restless, you will throw his yoke from off your neck."
>
> —GENESIS 27:1–40

One of the meanings to the word *blessing* is "to be favored by God." Jacob was once again willing to deceive in order to get what he wanted. He saw the importance of the birthright, which was his father's inheritance, and in some cases it was given to the firstborn son as a double portion. Not only did Jacob want his brother's birthright, but Jacob also wanted to be blessed by his father. The blessing that Isaac spoke over Jacob was a prophecy of what was to come, and it was a life of favor from God.

Little did Jacob know that in his scheming ways he would also inherit the promises and blessings given by God to Abraham. In Genesis 17:3–8, God tells Abram that he would be a father of many nations, that his name would no longer be Abram but Abraham, which means "a father of many," and that in his old age Abraham would be fruitful. Many nations and kings would come from him, and God would establish an everlasting covenant between him and his descendents after him for many generations.

God promised Abraham that the Messiah would come through his bloodline, and Jacob, in his quest for a blessing, inherited one of the greatest blessings in the

Word of God: to carry the seed that would later beget the King of kings and the Lord of lords.

Many in the church today are stale and rigid; they want everything to be the status quo. They want things to look a certain way, and as soon as they are taken out of the boxes they have put themselves and God in they think that "it's too much." The church and the world judge people that truly hunger and thirst after God as excessive, unbalanced, and unstable, and yet God loves that "Jacob kind of heart." He loves that Jacob was willing to do whatever it took to get his father's double portion and to be blessed.

God later changed Jacob's name to Israel and through Jacob produced the twelve tribes of Israel, which later brought Jesus Christ, our Messiah. After God renames someone in the Bible, that person is always called and referred to by their new name. (Abraham was no longer called Abram, Peter was no longer called Simon, and Paul was no longer Saul.) Like author Steve Thompson says in his book *You May All Prophesy!*, "The scripture could have read, 'Israel have I loved.' But God said that He loved Jacob, using the name indicative of the lusting, deceiving man that Jacob was prior to his nature being changed."[2] God was saying that He loved the man that deceived, not just the man that Jacob became.

The Bible says in Hebrews 12:16 (NLT), "Make sure that no one is immoral or godless like Esau, who traded his birthright as the firstborn son for a single meal." God found it to be very offensive that Esau thought so little of that which God had for him that he gave it away for a single meal. In the church there are those who look very put-together; things seem to look so good on the outside, but their hearts are far from God and they have become complacent in the things of God, just as Esau was. They don't want to search after God, because in finding Him, they may have to do things that are considered extreme in order to get all that God has for them. Those people would much rather give up all that God has for them—for far less then a bowl of soup. God loves and desires for people whose hearts are so sold out for Him that they are willing to do whatever it takes to get what God has for them, no matter what the cost!

I'm sure you know the story about David dancing before the Lord. Second Samuel 6:14–17, 20–23 says:

> Wearing a linen ephod, David was dancing before the LORD with all his might, while he and all Israel were bringing up the ark of the LORD with shouts and the sound of trumpets. As the ark of the LORD was entering the City of David, Michal daughter of Saul watched from a window. And when she saw King David leaping and dancing before the LORD, she despised him in her heart. They brought the ark of the LORD and set it in its place inside the tent that David had pitched for it, and David sacrificed burnt offerings and fellowship offerings before the LORD.... When David returned home to bless his household, Michal daughter of Saul came out to meet him and said, "How the king of Israel has distinguished himself today, going around half-naked in full view of the slave girls of his servants as any vulgar fellow would!" David said to Michal, "It was before the LORD, who chose me rather than your father or anyone from his house when he appointed me ruler over the LORD's people Israel—I will celebrate before

> the Lord. I will become even more undignified than this, and I will be humiliated in my own eyes. But by these slave girls you spoke of, I will be held in honor." And Michal daughter of Saul had no children to the day of her death.

So David, who God says is a man after His own heart, not only danced before the Lord, but it says he danced with all of his might and that he would do whatever it took to glorify God, including becoming more undignified and humiliating himself. The one person who despised David for this extreme act became barren and was never blessed with children after that. Unlike today's society, in the biblical days, children were one of the greatest blessings that a person could ever have, so she was literally never blessed again.

God hates the attitude of those who do not consider Him and who He is as being praiseworthy of their consideration and time. Again, Steve Thompson says in his book *You May All Prophesy!*:

> From the time of man's creation, God has desired to share His nature, glory, and power. This was his original intention. He has longed for those who would so hunger and thirst for His power, presence, anointing, authority, and blessing that they would pursue Him for it. Too many generations have been like Esau, despising the richness of God's blessing, and setting their hearts on temporary things, forfeiting the opportunity to share in His glory and power.

Sadly, these people are giving up having a wonderful relationship with their Creator just because it seemed a little risky, unorthodox, or extreme. They care more about what others will think of them than whether they get to that special place in God. They have compromised and accepted less than what God has for them, all because they were unwilling to step out in faith and run after God, no matter what it took or cost. Jacob ran after God in such a way that God blessed him and those after him. There is story after story of men and women in the Bible who pursued God in ways that were extreme, yet they are exalted because of it.

We all know that Jacob may have pursued God in the wrong ways, but the thing is, he still pursued Him! We all have character flaws that God has to work on. There is no perfect person. We all fall short of the glory of God, but He wants to refine us like gold, cleanse us, and make us worthy of the calling that He has on all of our lives. He wants all of us to pursue Him with all of our hearts. It's in pursuing Him that He can actually begin His work in us. God wants to have a wonderful relationship with each and every one of us. He is not a respecter of people. He loves everyone the same. Dick and Jane over there are no more worthy of God's love and grace than you are. He wants each and every one of us.

So, after Jacob deceived his brother, his mother told him to go to her people. On his way the Lord gave him a dream.

> And he dreamed, and behold a ladder set up on the earth, and the top of it reached to heaven: and behold the angels of God ascending and descending on it. And, behold, the Lord stood above it, and said, I am the Lord God of Abraham thy father, and the God of Isaac: the

> land whereon thou liest, to thee will I give it, and to thy seed; And thy seed shall be as the dust of the earth, and thou shalt spread abroad to the west, and to the east, and to the north, and to the south: and in thee and in thy seed shall all the families of the earth be blessed. And, behold, I am with thee, and will keep thee in all places whither thou goest, and will bring thee again into this land; for I will not leave thee, until I have done that which I have spoken to thee of. And Jacob awaked out of his sleep, and he said, Surely the Lord is in this place; and I knew it not. And he was afraid, and said, How dreadful is this place! this is none other but the house of God, and this is the gate of heaven. And Jacob rose up early in the morning, and took the stone that he had put for his pillows, and set it up for a pillar, and poured oil upon the top of it. And he called the name of that place Bethel: but the name of that city was called Luz at the first. And Jacob vowed a vow, saying, If God will be with me, and will keep me in this way that I go, and will give me bread to eat, and raiment to put on, So that I come again to my father's house in peace; then shall the Lord be my God: And this stone, which I have set for a pillar, shall be God's house: and of all that thou shalt give me I will surely give the tenth unto thee.
>
> —Genesis 28:12–22, kjv

First, God gives Jacob a promise through a dream. Then the refining begins. It seems in life that God gives some sort of promise or dream to a person before He really begins the refining process, just like He gave to Joseph. I believe He does this so that when we are going through the trials we will have hope to keep us going. God promises that He will never give us more than what we can handle and that He will also give us His peace and joy. (See 1 Corinthians 10:13; John 14:27; John 15:11.) Jacob was forced to undergo many trials, including marrying the wrong woman. In order to get to marry the one he loved and was originally promised he had to live under his father-in-law for many years. The Bible says we will reap what we sow; it doesn't matter who we are. Jacob sowed deceit, and he later reaped deceit when his own uncle deceived him into marrying his oldest daughter instead of his youngest daughter, whom he originally promised to Jacob. But even in his trials, the Lord was with him and even blessed him. He actually blessed Jacob so much that his own father-in-law became jealous. When you are pursuing God and doing His will, God will begin to bless your life, and in many cases people will become jealous of the blessings that God has given to you. Malachi 1:2—"I have loved Jacob, but Esau I have hated"—really shows that God is more pleased with the kind of person who pursues God in any way versus the person who looks at the things of God as trivial.

Here is a man who did all he could and whatever it took just to be blessed by God, and he found favor because of it. God took this man and matured him through trials, and when the Lord had matured Him enough God not only restored his relationships but He blessed him beyond his wildest dreams.

In Genesis 32:24–30 we read one of my favorite stories in the Bible.

> So Jacob was left alone, and a man wrestled with him till daybreak. When the man saw that he could not overpower him, he touched the socket of Jacob's hip so that his hip was wrenched as he wrestled with the man. Then the man said, "Let me go, for it is daybreak." But Jacob replied, "I will not let you go unless you bless me." The man asked him, "What is your name?" "Jacob," he answered. Then the man said, "Your name will no longer be Jacob, but Israel, because you have struggled with God and with humans and have overcome." Jacob said, "Please tell me your name." But he replied, "Why do you ask my name?" Then he blessed him there. So Jacob called the place Peniel, saying, "It is because I saw God face to face, and yet my life was spared."

Jacob wanted God's blessings and approval so much he actually got to wrestle with Him. How incredible to be able to wrestle with God Almighty! I have always been amazed at the kind of drive that Jacob must have had to get to wrestle with God. And not only did Jacob wrestle with God until God blessed him, but then he even asked God for more by asking God what His name was. Jacob knew whom he wrestled with, yet he wanted God to tell him His name. The drive that Jacob had was the same drive that caused him to lie, deceive, and wrestle throughout his entire life, and that is what God loved so much about him.

The entire Bible is written about people who were extraordinary or unusually excellent and who deserve our attention because of being wonderfully different—and the Bible is also written about people who were the complete opposite, people who did everything but bring glory to God. I believe God did that purposely so that we could study those people's lives and have an example of how to live and how not to live.

Out of the extraordinary men and women that the Bible talks about, they all have four things in common.

The first is that they all had their faults, from adultery, like David, to pride, like Joseph. We all fall short of the glory of God. We all sin.

The second is that they all went through trials as God perfected them, matured them, and refined them, like Moses in the desert and Jonah in the belly of the fish. These men and women were no different than any other human in the world in the fact that they still had sin in their lives and they still needed to be made more mature in God so that God could trust them with His works. Just like you wouldn't send a child into the world without some sort of maturing, God doesn't want His people unprepared. There is literally a war going on out there, and He wants us not only prepared but effective. He wants to do that with every one of us. He wants to cleanse and refine all of us so that He can use and trust us with all that He has for us, but we have to be willing to go through that process of being purified. Being refined is not easy, and it will hurt our flesh. Jesus said we were to crucify our flesh daily. Does that sound easy or painless?

Quite a few years ago I was going through some really tough stuff. The trials were really overwhelming, as God was really beginning to refine me and make me more mature in Christ. Someone told me that if a shepherd has a lamb that has a tendency to wander off, to save that lamb from being hurt or even killed the shepherd will break one of the lamb's legs, and in doing this the shepherd is then forced to carry the lamb until its leg is healed. By being forced to carry this lamb everywhere, the lamb and the shepherd will form an incredible bond, and when the lamb is finally healed, because of the bond they share, that lamb will never wander off again. Although that may seem extreme to some, to me it was a great comfort. I knew then that every trial was going to bring me closer to my God, just as labor pains bring a women closer to meeting her baby. Just as the pains of child labor are worth it, so are the trials we endure for the sake of getting closer to a wonderful God.

The third thing that these men and women have in common is that the men and women loved God with their whole hearts, no matter their faults. They were all willing to give up everything for the God that they loved, including disobeying a law that went against God, knowing that the punishment was that they would be thrown into a fire or into a den of lions. In exploring the lives of every one of these men and women, we will find their great, uncompromising, furious, and wild love for God. Abraham was not only willing to give up His only son but also the promise that came with him.

And the fourth reason is that because these people allowed God to refine them. Because of their great love for God, God was then able to use them in incredible ways to glorify Him, using them to save entire nations, to heal the sick, and raise the dead. And the blessings on these people's lives were more than most can imagine. It's interesting; one of the definitions of the word *blessing* is actually "approval." Don't we all long to have approval from God? How much are you willing to do to get it? Without our willingness to be melted and molded into God's likeness, He will never be able to use us in the great and mighty ways that He desires.

The difference between Jacob and Esau couldn't be plainer, but it really comes down to one thing: Jacob desired God and the blessings of God, and Esau didn't, and their actions followed.

Jesus says in Revelation 3:15–22:

> "I know your deeds, that you are neither cold nor hot. I wish you were either one or the other! So, because you are lukewarm—neither hot nor cold—I am about to spit you out of my mouth. You say, 'I am rich; I have acquired wealth and do not need a thing.' But you do not realize that you are wretched, pitiful, poor, blind and naked. I counsel you to buy from me gold refined in the fire, so you can become rich; and white clothes to wear, so you can cover your shameful nakedness; and salve to put on your eyes, so you can see. Those whom I love I rebuke and discipline. So be earnest and repent. Here I am! I stand at the door and knock. If anyone hears my voice and opens the door, I will come in and eat with that person, and they with me. To the one who is victorious, I will give the right to sit with me on my throne, just as I was victorious and sat down with my Father on his throne. Whoever has ears, let them hear what the Spirit says to the churches."

How powerful is that? God wants us on fire for Him. He wants us *hot*! The word *hot* has thirty-three meanings. A few of those meanings are "causing controversy, dangerous, intense, exciting, enthusiastically eager, and desire." He wants us to cause controversy in our love for

Him. He wants us to live on the edge for Him. He wants us to enthusiastically, eagerly desire Him with a great intensity.

Revelation also says that He stands at the door and knocks. He wants the church to answer so that He can come in and dine with us. He wants us to push through those trials for His name's sake so that we may be overcomers.

God doesn't tell us that life will be easy, but He does promise that if we search for Him, He will be found; and if we ask of Him, He will give; and if we knock, the door will be opened. Marriage, children, work, and life in general are hard. Paul said in 2 Corinthians 4:8–9, "We are hard pressed on every side, but not crushed; perplexed, but not in despair; persecuted, but not abandoned; struck down, but not destroyed." Life is hard, but God wants us to push through the difficult trials and continue to seek Him with our whole hearts, trusting in Him with every aspect of our lives. Through the struggle and the wrestling matches, if we don't grow faint in doing good He will bless us beyond our wildest dreams.

2

DAVID VS. SAUL

Trust God In All Things

Trust in the Lord with all your heart and lean not on your own understanding; in all your ways submit to him, and he will make your paths straight.

—Proverbs 3:5–6

WHEN SAMUEL THE prophet grew old he appointed his sons as judges over Israel. But his sons did not walk in his ways. They turned aside after dishonest gain and accepted bribes and perverted justice, so the elders of Israel got together and went to Samuel and told him that they wanted a king to lead them. This displeased Samuel, so he prayed to the Lord. And the Lord told him that the people did not reject him (Samuel) but instead rejected God as their King. So, God told Samuel to listen to them and give them a king but to also warn them and let them know what a king over them would do. (See 1 Samuel 8:1–9.)

From the beginning of time all God has wanted was to bless His people and to know them personally, revealing His love and personality to His people. He wants to walk and talk with us as Friend, Father, and King. But the people in David's time didn't want that. They wanted to have what other nations had; they wanted to do things their way and to only use God when it was convenient for them.

We've all heard the saying that "one bad apple will ruin a bunch." It's a true statement. God knows that the influence of evil is strong. That's why He tells us, "Bad company corrupts good character" (1 Cor. 15:33). God has, from the beginning of time, tried to protect His people from the influence of Satan. Satan is a liar and a deceiver. Satan will do whatever it takes to imprison every person on this earth, so God has tried to keep His people from conforming to this world and its thoughts and ideals.

> And be not conformed to this world: but be ye transformed by the renewing of your mind, that ye may prove what is that good, and acceptable, and perfect, will of God.
>
> —Romans 12:2, kjv

God knew that giving the people a king would not do anything for them. What He really wanted was for the people to trust Him to rule over them.

Many times God will give a person what they want, even though God has continually warned them that it is not the best for them. People want what is easiest.

I saw a commercial on TV where they showed an "easy button." I don't remember the details, but when something was difficult they said something to the effect of, "Wouldn't it be nice to have an easy button in life, so when something is hard you just push the button, and *voila.* It's easy and done." The only problem with this kind of thinking is that we have become an "easy button" society. We as a society have tried so hard to make our lives easier that we are now missing out on all the blessings that come with pushing through those difficult times in life. Our society no longer has integrity, and we no longer have the will to do what's right because it's too hard.

If marriage is hard, our culture tells us, "It's OK. Just get a divorce." When a woman becomes pregnant and realizes she doesn't want those responsibilities yet, she just goes out and gets an abortion, killing not only the life within her but the blessing that God Almighty wanted to give her. When a woman goes through labor she wants drugs or some kind of pain relief instead of pushing through the pain and getting to see the glory. The "easy button" is everywhere in life. But it's only a trick of the devil. He wants to steal the blessings that God wants for us. Satan makes this "easy button" look so nice, when in fact it's a lie from the pit of hell. God knew there would be trials in life, and all He wants is for us to push through and come out the other side more mature and blessed. If marriage is hard, and I can guarantee that it will be, God wants you to stick with it and go through the trials, and I promise you that if you do, you will be blessed.

I was eighteen when I got married, and my husband was nineteen. We were very immature and really knew nothing about how a marriage was supposed to work. We didn't know how to communicate in any way, and from the beginning I believed God Almighty had sent me on a mission to change my husband in any way that

I could. I knew that he would be the perfect man if only he would do as I wanted. We were both very stubborn, so I'm sure you can imagine what our marriage looked like. He golfed, and I fought. What I didn't realize was that I wasn't fighting Satan like I originally thought, but instead I was fighting God and my husband. Praise God, divorce wasn't an option in either of our minds (probably because we were both too stubborn), or I wouldn't be sitting here telling you the testimony of God's grace.

I love God with my whole heart, and I seek Him every single day. I know God and trust Him with everything in my life, including my heart. I think it's easy to trust God with most things, but as people who have been hurt before, trusting Him with our heart has to be the hardest. I am willing to do whatever it is that He wants me to do. I know that God will take care of me, and even if it hurts my flesh for a season, I know He knows what's best for me. This is what got me through the first few years of my marriage. Life was hard. I was lonely; I felt like I was the only one who was going through the kind of trials that I was going through. I was hard pressed on every side, and it's hard when you're in the midst of trials to realize that even though you're hard pressed, you're not crushed. I was confused about what was going on and wondering if things were ever going to change, but I was never left without hope.

Even in my loneliness I was never really abandoned or on my own. God never leaves us or forsakes us. During those few years, I constantly cried out to God. I tried to listen to what He told my heart and was willing to do what He wanted me to do. I spent every day in the Word. During those first few years I spent every second of every day dying to my flesh, and God delivered me from anger, bitterness, hatred, unforgiveness, condemnation, jealously, self-pity, and I'm sure many other things.

Somewhere during those first years, after crying out to God, I remember being in a Christian bookstore when this book jumped out at me. The name of the book was *Is There a Moose in Your Marriage?* (renamed *The Politically Incorrect Wife*).[1] I grabbed the book off of the shelves and thought to myself, "Praise God! Finally God has answered my prayers. Of course there is a moose in my marriage, and his name is Mr. Rory Wolff." So I bought the book. Finally I was going to get the help I needed, and my husband would finally be the husband I knew he should be.

The book started out talking about how in Alaska once in a while a large moose will walk onto the road and just sit there. If you are trying to drive somewhere there is really no way to get the moose out of the way. Not only are they dangerous, but I doubt most moose are going to listen to you honk your horn. I sat there reading the book with a goofy grin on my face, thinking, "I know this book was written for me; and boy, she must know my husband." The book continued on, and I soon realized that the author wasn't referring to my husband as being the moose but me! This came as a bit of a shock. You see, up until this point I had blamed him, his parents, and everyone else for the problems in our marriage, never really realizing that it takes two to make a marriage and two to break a marriage. Sure, he had as many issues as I did, but I soon came to perceive that no matter what, I will never be able to change anyone but myself. And even in changing myself I came to understand that I really couldn't even do that on my own. I needed God's help. We are unable to do anything without God, but with God we can do all things through Him who gives us strength (Phil. 4:13). It was still very tempting to try to change him, but in changing myself and dying to my flesh, I changed.

When I finally changed and God delivered me from sins, past hurts, wrong ways of thinking, and many other bondages, for the first time I was happy, clean, and free, and I no longer had to have the control, because I knew that God was in control. I knew that if God was the one in control all would be well. This didn't happen overnight. Everything in life is a process and a season. Just as most people aren't instantly transformed after they have accepted Christ as their Lord and Savior, most people aren't instantly healed or delivered. I finally got to a point where I no longer had the need to change my husband. I wasn't 100 percent satisfied with him, but I knew God would do a much better job than me. It was at this point in my life that my husband started to change, as did our marriage. He started to trust me and really love me, and we started to grow into one flesh. It was never easy, but it was a million times worth it to lay down my hurts, sins, pain, and even my husband on the throne and let God take the burden and fix it all.

There were many verses in the Word that I clung to during those trials. One of them was Ephesians 3:20, "Now to him who is able to do immeasurably more than all we ask or imagine." Just think—how amazing!—God is promising us that if we trust Him and believe Him, He will give us more than we ask for and imagine. In fact, He will give us immeasurably (without measure) more.

I think it's rough for Americans to get married because we are so used to having everything that we want. We are selfish, and we have these incorrect expectations. We enter into marriage and soon realize it's not what we first thought, and then we want out. When I first got married it only took a week for me to realize that it was no honeymoon. I prayed to God and asked Him, "Why, after all the years of praying for the perfect husband and marriage, did You not give them to me?" I actually felt mad at God, like He had tricked me or had allowed Satan to trick me. But I clearly heard Him say that, like everything in life, if something is just given to you without any effort or work, not only will it not be worth as much to you but you will take it for granted. He really was answering my prayers, just not in the way I thought He would. He wanted me to have the best marriage, and He wanted me to hold it in high regard and never to take it for granted, but in order for that to happen I had to work for it.

Once I got my old ways of thinking out of the way I used to imagine Rory and I happily married. I would tell God my thoughts in detail. I would tell Him that I imagined that I would one day be a great vessel for Him to use and trust, and that I would be the woman of God that He created me to be. I imagined Rory and I would have the best marriage. We would be able to communicate. Rory would love me, and we'd have children, which at this time Rory didn't want.

I would dream out loud to God all of the time. I always made sure my thoughts were in line with His Word and His will for my life. Then I would tell God, "I imagine really big, God, but You promise to do immeasurably more than I ask or imagine." Speaking is one of the greatest keys to getting what God has for you. It's also one of the biggest keys to getting what Satan has for you. God spoke the earth into existence. There is so much power in our words, more than we even realize. I could write an entire book on the power of our words and the importance of what we speak, because the Bible talks so much about it.

> The tongue has the power of life and death, and those that love it will eat its fruit.
>
> —Proverbs 18:21

My life isn't perfect, and I'm still imagining really big, believing God for bigger, but God has done exactly as He has promised. He has taken me to heights beyond anything I could have dreamed. He has restored my marriage, given me a wonderful husband, seven beautiful children whom Rory adores, and has changed me in the process. I still need a lot of changing. My heart isn't always right. I still struggle with selfishness, I'm impatient in life and sometimes toward my children, and I struggle with how to balance my time in a fashion that glorifies God; but I know I am still a work in progress, and someday these and many other hidden sins will be taken from my life. I will continue day by day to grow closer to God through it all. I was willing to press through the hard things in life and was tremendously blessed because of it.

Now Israel wanted to be like other nations and wanted a king, even though God had bigger plans for Israel. God wanted Israel to trust Him to be their King so that He could take care of them and bless them, but their flesh overrode their desire to trust God and do what

He thought was best. So, God gave them a king. He appointed Saul as king over Israel, and the people soon realized their mistake in not trusting God and repented, and God forgave them. (See 1 Samuel 10:17–24; 11:12–12:25.) That's the best part: we all sin and fall short, we all take the easy road at one time or another in our lives, but God is always there waiting to bring us back, forgive us, and bless us.

In studying the lives of David and Saul it doesn't take much to realize the difference between these two people. At first God used Saul, and I believe that Saul's heart was even right. The Bible tells us in 1 Samuel 10 that the Spirit of the Lord came upon Saul, and he prophesied. Even to this day there are some who wonder if Saul wasn't one of the prophets. So, not only did God's power come upon him, but he was even humble about it. When Saul's uncle asked him what Samuel said to him, Saul didn't brag to his uncle and tell him that God's power came upon him, he prophesied, and that Samuel told him that God wanted him to be king. Not many people could keep that a secret, yet Saul did. The interesting thing about most of the people in the Bible, and even today in the church, is most really did and do believe in God and to a point want to please Him. They just want to please Him on their terms, kind of like Cain and his offering.

The first mistake Saul did as king is found in 1 Samuel 13:3–14.

> Jonathan attacked the Philistine outpost at Geba, and the Philistines heard about it. Then Saul had the trumpet blown throughout the land and said, "Let the Hebrews hear!" So all Israel heard

the news: "Saul has attacked the Philistine outpost, and now Israel has become obnoxious to the Philistines." And the people were summoned to join Saul at Gilgal. The Philistines assembled to fight Israel, with three thousand chariots, six thousand charioteers, and soldiers as numerous as the sand on the seashore. They went up and camped at Mikmash, east of Beth Aven. When the Israelites saw that their situation was critical and that their army was hard pressed, they hid in caves and thickets, among the rocks, and in pits and cisterns. Some Hebrews even crossed the Jordan to the land of Gad and Gilead. Saul remained at Gilgal, and all the troops with him were quaking with fear. He waited seven days, the time set by Samuel; but Samuel did not come to Gilgal, and Saul's men began to scatter. So he said, "Bring me the burnt offering and the fellowship offerings." And Saul offered up the burnt offering. Just as he finished making the offering, Samuel arrived, and Saul went out to greet him. "What have you done?" asked Samuel. Saul replied, "When I saw that the men were scattering, and that you did not come at the set time, and that the Philistines were assembling at Mikmash, I thought, 'Now the Philistines will come down against me at Gilgal, and I have not sought the Lord's favor.' So I felt compelled to offer the burnt offering." "You have done a foolish thing," Samuel said. "You have not kept the command the Lord your God gave you; if you had, he would have established your kingdom over Israel for all time. But now your kingdom will not endure; the Lord has sought out a man after his own heart and

> appointed him ruler of his people, because you have not kept the LORD's command."

The people were all afraid, and Saul followed suit. God doesn't want us to believe with what our eyes see or what our ears hear. He wants us to have faith in Him and trust Him. Saul was moved by his senses. He decided not to trust God and to take matters into his own hands, and it cost him his kingship.

It's hard when everything in the natural realm says one thing and the Word of God says another. It's hard when your body feels sick, but the Word of God says, "By his wounds you have been healed" (1 Pet. 2:24). God wants us to know Him so well that we believe Him over what everything else in the natural realm says. He is our Father, and He always knows best.

The second mistake Saul made as king is found in 1 Samuel 15:1–35. God had spoken through Samuel to Saul, telling Saul that He (God) was going to punish the Amalekites for what they did to Israel. God wanted Saul to totally destroy the entire race of Amalekites, along with all of their belongings. God didn't want anything or anyone spared. But instead of obeying God, Saul decided to do things his own way. He not only spared king Agag but also the best of the sheep and cattle.

> Then the word of the LORD came to Samuel: "I regret that I have made Saul king, because he has turned away from me and has not carried out my instructions." Samuel was angry, and he cried out to the LORD all that night. Early in the morning Samuel got up and went to meet Saul, but he was told, "Saul has gone to Carmel. There he has set up a monument in his own honor and

has turned and gone on down to Gilgal." When Samuel reached him, Saul said, "The Lord bless you! I have carried out the Lord's instructions." But Samuel said, "What then is this bleating of sheep in my ears? What is this lowing of cattle that I hear?" Saul answered, "The soldiers brought them from the Amalekites; they spared the best of the sheep and cattle to sacrifice to the Lord your God, but we totally destroyed the rest." "Enough!" Samuel said to Saul. "Let me tell you what the Lord said to me last night." "Tell me," Saul replied. Samuel said, "Although you were once small in your own eyes, did you not become the head of the tribes of Israel? The Lord anointed you king over Israel. And he sent you on a mission, saying, 'Go and completely destroy those wicked people, the Amalekites; wage war against them until you have wiped them out.' Why did you not obey the Lord? Why did you pounce on the plunder and do evil in the eyes of the Lord?" "But I did obey the Lord," Saul said. "I went on the mission the Lord assigned me. I completely destroyed the Amalekites and brought back Agag their king. The soldiers took sheep and cattle from the plunder, the best of what was devoted to God, in order to sacrifice them to the Lord your God at Gilgal." But Samuel replied: "Does the Lord delight in burnt offerings and sacrifices as much as in obeying the Lord? To obey is better than sacrifice, and to heed is better than the fat of rams. For rebellion is like the sin of divination, and arrogance like the evil of idolatry. Because you have rejected the word of the Lord, he has rejected you as king." Then Saul said to Samuel,

"I have sinned. I violated the LORD's command and your instructions. I was afraid of the men and so I gave in to them. Now I beg you, forgive my sin and come back with me, so that I may worship the LORD." But Samuel said to him, "I will not go back with you. You have rejected the word of the LORD, and the LORD has rejected you as king over Israel!" As Samuel turned to leave, Saul caught hold of the hem of his robe, and it tore. Samuel said to him, "The LORD has torn the kingdom of Israel from you today and has given it to one of your neighbors—to one better than you. He who is the Glory of Israel does not lie or change his mind; for he is not a human being, that he should change his mind." Saul replied, "I have sinned. But please honor me before the elders of my people and before Israel; come back with me, so that I may worship the LORD your God." So Samuel went back with Saul, and Saul worshiped the LORD. Then Samuel said, "Bring me Agag king of the Amalekites." Agag came to him in chains. And he thought, "Surely the bitterness of death is past." But Samuel said, "As your sword has made women childless, so will your mother be childless among women." And Samuel put Agag to death before the LORD at Gilgal. Then Samuel left for Ramah, but Saul went up to his home in Gibeah of Saul. Until the day Samuel died, he did not go to see Saul again, though Samuel mourned for him. And the LORD regretted that he had made Saul king over Israel.

—1 SAMUEL 15:10–35

Not only did Saul not carry out the instructions of God the way that he was supposed to, but he truly did not seem to find anything wrong with the way that he did things. Saul made it seem that what he was doing was honorable. He told Samuel that the reason that he disobeyed God was to save the best, so that he could sacrifice them to the Lord.

The Bible says that Saul was once small in his own eyes. The key word here is *once*. Pride is an awful sin because it blinds people. Saul was once humble, but now he was prideful. In pride Saul kept Agag alive, set up a monument in his own honor, couldn't admit his wrongdoing, and wanted to be honored before men. His heart wasn't right, and he believed he knew better than God. We all make mistakes, which God is always quick to forgive, but Saul didn't have so much a sin issue as a wrong heart. He didn't care if God truly forgave him; he cared more about what it would look like to the people and what would become of his throne. He not only rejected God by disobeying his Word but rejected God in his heart.

Then we have David. David was a man after God's own heart. The Lord sent Samuel to the house of Jesse to anoint one of his sons to be king. When Samuel got there and saw Jesse's sons, one of them named Eliab, he thought, "'Surely the LORD's anointed stands here before the LORD.' But the LORD said to Samuel, 'Do not consider his appearance or his height, for I have rejected him. The LORD does not look at the things people look at. People look at the outward appearance, but the LORD looks at the heart'" (1 Sam. 16:6–7). The wonderful thing about God is, unlike the world, He doesn't care about our appearances or what we've accomplished according to human standards. God only cares about our heart. He wanted a king that truly cared about Him, because God knew if the king loved Him, he would obey God and would have the best interest of the people at heart. So David went before Samuel, "Then the LORD said, 'Rise and anoint him; he is the one.' So Samuel took the horn of oil and anointed him in the presence of his brothers, and from that day on the Spirit of the LORD came upon David in power" (1 Sam. 16:12–13).

You see, when you have a heart after God He will anoint you with His power so that you can bless others with it. Being a king isn't a place of honor as much as it is a place of servanthood. God wants us to serve Him and His people.

David didn't start out being king. He was anointed for the position, but the position wasn't his until God had made him ready. He still had to have things ironed out in his own life before God could truly use him the way that He wanted to. So God sent David to serve Saul. When God is ironing things out in our lives He will normally send us to places that are very unpleasant, and it's in learning to live in those situations that we mature and get to the place where God can and will use us.

Before David began serving Saul, there was a champion fighter who was over nine feet tall named Goliath. Goliath was a Philistine who would go before the people of Israel every day and shout:

> "Why do you come out and line up for battle? Am I not a Philistine, and are you not the servants of Saul? Choose a man and have him come down to me. If he is able to fight and kill me, we will become your subjects; but if I overcome him

> and kill him, you will become our subjects and serve us." Then the Philistine said, "This day I defy the armies of Israel! Give me a man and let us fight each other." On hearing the Philistine's words, Saul and all the Israelites were dismayed and terrified.
>
> —1 Samuel 17:8–11

This angered David and he said, "Who is this uncircumcised Philistine that he should defy the armies of the living God?" (1 Sam. 17:26). David told Saul not to lose heart, that he would go and fight Goliath. Saul told David that he wasn't able to go against the Philistine because he was just a boy. But David said to Saul that while keeping his father's sheep he had fought and killed lion and bear, and just as he had "killed both the lion and the bear; this uncircumcised Philistine will be like one of them, because he has defied the armies of the living God. The Lord who rescued me from the paw of the lion and the paw of the bear will rescue me from the hand of this Philistine" (1 Sam. 17:36–37).

So, without wearing any tunic, which was like a military uniform, or any coat of armor or helmet on his head and without any sword, David chose five smooth stones from a stream and went against a champion fighting giant. Can you imagine? Here is a boy without any armor, sword, or any other form of protection going to fight against a giant, all because this giant spoke against the armies of the living God. Not only does David have great zeal and passion for his God but also great trust in his God's ability to protect him.

God wants us to trust Him in such a way that even in the physical realm, where what we are fighting seems impossible, we believe His promises to see us through it. My husband calls it "wholehearted abandonment." This is when we abandon every natural thing to wholeheartedly chase after the supernatural. This is what God desires for us to have, to trust Him so completely that we wholeheartedly abandon all of our thoughts, emotions, and ideals and leave all to follow after Him—and when we do our lives will never be the same. If we do not wholeheartedly abandon all we know to follow after Almighty God, He cannot work tangibly in our lives in the way that He desires.

David knew God and had seen God work in his life before. He knew that God had protected Him from the lion and the bear and had promised him that he would one day be king over Israel, so he knew that God would again protect him. He didn't have the whole plan laid out on exactly what to do. God doesn't ask us to plan but only to trust. Many times we want to see a plan of everything that God asks of us, but where is the trust in that? He wants us to have blind trust. When a father throws a child into the air, the child isn't scared that they will be dropped, because they know their daddy and trust him. God is our Daddy. He is our Father. His love for us is greater than any human love.

So here's little David, going before the champion fighting Goliath, and Goliath actually, in his pride, gets offended. He can't believe that the armies of Israel would actually send a boy to fight him.

First Samuel 17:43–51 (KJV) says:

> And the Philistine said unto David, Am I a dog, that thou comest to me with staves? And the Philistine cursed David by his gods. And the

> Philistine said to David, Come to me, and I will give thy flesh unto the fowls of the air, and to the beasts of the field. Then said David to the Philistine, Thou comest to me with a sword, and with a spear, and with a shield: but I come to thee in the name of the LORD of hosts, the God of the armies of Israel, whom thou hast defied. This day will the LORD deliver thee into mine hand; and I will smite thee, and take thine head from thee; and I will give the carcases of the host of the Philistines this day unto the fowls of the air, and to the wild beasts of the earth; that all the earth may know that there is a God in Israel. And all this assembly shall know that the LORD saveth not with sword and spear: for the battle is the LORD's, and he will give you into our hands. And it came to pass, when the Philistine arose, and came, and drew nigh to meet David, that David hastened, and ran toward the army to meet the Philistine. And David put his hand in his bag, and took thence a stone, and slang it, and smote the Philistine in his forehead, that the stone sunk into his forehead; and he fell upon his face to the earth. So David prevailed over the Philistine with a sling and with a stone, and smote the Philistine, and slew him; but there was no sword in the hand of David. Therefore David ran, and stood upon the Philistine, and took his sword, and drew it out of the sheath thereof, and slew him, and cut off his head therewith. And when the Philistines saw their champion was dead, they fled.

How amazing! David loved God so much that it angered him that any would defy God's army. And then he not only trusted God to protect him but to triumph over the Philistine army. David stood before Goliath in the name of God Almighty and won a great victory. We can all stand in the face of our Goliaths and take victory in God's name. I especially love the part where David says to Goliath, "You come against me with sword and spear and javelin, but I come against you in the name of the LORD Almighty, the God of the armies of Israel, whom you have defied" (1 Sam. 17:45). How powerful!

Another amazing thing is, David said in 1 Samuel 17:47, "All those gathered here will know that it is not by sword or spear that the LORD saves; for the battle is the LORD's, and he will give all of you into our hands." We see two things here. The first is not only trust but humility on David's part. He was not about to take the glory from God, but he made sure that everyone knew that he, David, wasn't the one defeating the giant, but God was.

The second is that God goes before us. In Deuteronomy 31:8 it says, "The LORD himself goes before you and will be with you; he will never leave you nor forsake you. Do not be afraid; do not be discouraged." Life is hard, but God wants us to know that everything is taken care of. He goes before us to prepare the way for us. The battle should be ours, but it's not! We all should be hell-bound, but Jesus Christ paid the price, and those of us that believe in Him and have a personal relationship with Him will no longer have to fight the battle alone. God is not only with us, never leaving us, but He has made our battles His. He will fight with us, and with Him fighting alongside us the victory is always ours. All we have to do is trust Him.

David wasn't perfect, and to some he probably did

even more wrong on the outside then Saul. David stole another man's wife, got her pregnant, and then killed the woman's husband to cover his tracks. This sounds worse than what Saul did, but because David's heart was right before God and Saul's wasn't it made all the difference. Trust is an amazing thing. The word *faith* means "belief, trust, and loyalty." The Bible says that without faith or trust in God we cannot please God (Heb. 11:6), we cannot move mountains (Matt. 21:21), we cannot be made whole (Mark 5:34), God can never calm the storms in our lives (Luke 8:25), our hearts will never be pure (Acts 15:9), we will never do any wonders or miracle (Acts 6:8), we will never be justified or accepted (Rom. 10:17), we can never be saved (Rom. 10:9), and we can never be healed (too many verses to put). Without faith and trust in God our lives will always be in shambles. Life is just not worth living if we cannot trust God and believe in Him and His love for us.

How do we learn to trust God? The Bible says that faith comes by hearing the Word of God (Rom. 10:17). God is His Word, and if you want a relationship with any person you need to know them and fellowship with them. Read God's Word; that's how you will begin to know Him, fall in love with Him, trust Him, and watch your life be transformed. Because God is not a respecter of people, having a personal relationship with the King of kings is for anyone who wants it—anyone who is willing to know and trust Him.

3

ABEL VS. CAIN

Give God Your Best

Give, and it will be given to you. A good measure, pressed down, shaken together and running over, will be poured into your lap. For with the measure you use, it will be measured to you.

—LUKE 6:38

WE'VE ALL HEARD stories about people who spend their whole lives hoarding their possessions. I heard about a man who had no one and was all alone. This man was found dead in his apartment many days after he had died. His apartment was bare of any real possessions. The man had starved to death. But when going through his apartment they found a stockpile of money. I don't remember the exact amount, but it was an incredible amount to have in cash hidden in a home, especially when the man had starved to death. While trying to find this exact story on the Internet, I found many more sad stories like it.

One of the stories that I read told about another man who lived in an old shack. He was found almost dead from starvation. In his clothes he had over twenty thousand dollars, and a further search of his house revealed more. He also owned several pieces of farmland. He only allowed himself eighty cents a week for food.

Another story told of a seventy-six-year-old woman who had also starved herself to death to keep from spending her money. On her they found one hundred and fifty dollars, and in the bank she had several thousand.

These stories are so sad. Greed isn't a new epidemic. The word *greed* means "a strong and overwhelming desire to have more of something, such as money, than is actually needed." The last chapter was a lot about trust, which is just another word for faith. The opposite of faith is fear. People who hoard are not only greedy, but they are afraid and fearful that if they don't save everything or save all of their money, then something will happen to them. Their material possessions not only bring them comfort, but they become their god.

The Bible actually talks a lot about money, and not much of it's good. It's OK to have money and to be rich as long as the money doesn't have you. God wants us to prosper, to have nice things, and to be without debt. They say Solomon was the richest person to ever live. God gave him his wealth, because it wasn't wealth that he asked for but wisdom. God told Solomon that he could have anything he wanted, and Solomon asked for wisdom so that he could serve and govern God's people while he was king. God was very pleased that Solomon asked for this instead of long life, wealth, or the death of an enemy, so God not only made him the wisest man, unlike any other, but also the richest. God also said He would give him honor, and, if He obeyed God, long life

(1 Kings 3:5–14). God wants to bless us, but He doesn't want us to gain the whole world and lose our souls in the process (Matt. 16:26).

The Bible says in 1 Timothy 6:7, 9–10, "For we brought nothing into the world, and we can take nothing out of it.... Those who want to get rich fall into temptation and a trap and into many foolish and harmful desires that plunge people into ruin and destruction. For the love of money is a root of all kinds of evil." You hear a lot of people say that money is the root to all evil, which isn't correct. It's the love of money that is a root to all kinds of evil. Most crimes seem to go hand in hand with the love of money.

Shortly after the fall of man, in which Adam and Eve disobeyed God, they began to reap what they had sown. They had two sons, one named Cain and another named Abel.

> Now Abel kept flocks, and Cain worked the soil. In the course of time Cain brought some of the fruits of the soil as an offering to the LORD. And Abel also brought an offering—fat portions from some of the firstborn of his flock. The LORD looked with favor on Abel and his offering, but on Cain and his offering he did not look with favor. So Cain was very angry, and his face was downcast.
>
> —GENESIS 4:2–5

Once again God is comparing two people and their hearts. Each brother brought a gift to the Lord. It doesn't say that God was mad at Cain for the gift that he brought, but it says that He didn't look at Cain or his offering with favor. The word *favor* means "preference" or "desire."

In the verse it says that God didn't favor Cain and his offering. God is once again looking at the heart of man. God knows man's heart. He knows our intentions and our innermost thoughts. He knew that Cain's heart wasn't right and that there was greed in his heart. Cain intentionally didn't give God his best. He gave God his leftovers. He didn't think that God was worth the best that he had. Abel, on the other hand, gave God his best. It says that Abel brought God the fat portions from some of his firstborn. The fat portion symbolizes the richest part of the animal, or the fattest of the flock. Abel brought God his very best. When Abel brought the Lord the firstborn, he was actually bringing God his firstfruits.

Let's say there is a person who doesn't make a lot of money and lives on a budget, and that person only gets paid once a month, at the beginning of the month. That person will sit down at the beginning of every month and decide where every penny of his or her money goes. Now, the world wants you to think of the things that could take place—car accidents, out of work, getting sick, etc. But God wants you to think of Him and trust Him. He wants you to first give to Him, acknowledging that the money that you are given is actually from Him. Then He wants what you have left to be put toward living expenses, not the other way around. God doesn't want your leftovers. That is your firstfruit. It's trusting God with what He has given to you; it's the best and most important. And when we trust Him, He will never let us down.

Firstfruits aren't all about the money. It also has to do

with life. God always wants your best, but He especially wants you to once again trust Him and have faith in Him. Firstfruits are so important to God that He actually has a holiday or a feast, called the Feast of Tabernacles, which is an acknowledgement that the fruits of the harvest are from Him. (See Exodus 23:16; 34:22.)

So, Abel not only trusted the Lord with his firstfruits and acknowledged that they were from the Lord, but he gave God his best. He honored God by showing God respect and admiration, whereas Cain didn't. Cain, in his greed, decided to disrespect the Lord's gift. He didn't love the Lord enough to give Him his first and best. This is why the Lord didn't find favor with Cain or with his gift. God could see his heart and knew all that was in it. Giving God a poor gift wasn't a sin, but it showed a poor heart condition that could turn into sin if left unchecked. Like the verse in 1 Timothy 6:9 says, "Those who want to get rich fall into temptation and a trap and into many foolish and harmful desires that plunge people into ruin and destruction." God loved Cain and didn't want the greed in his heart to turn into sin, and He knew that if Cain didn't clean out his heart, that sin was lurking around the corner waiting to overtake him.

> Then the LORD said to Cain, "Why are you angry? Why is your face downcast? If you do what is right, will you not be accepted? But if you do not do what is right, sin is crouching at your door; it desires to have you, but you must rule over it." Now Cain said to his brother Abel, "Let's go out to the field." While they were in the field, Cain attacked his brother Abel and killed him. Then the LORD said to Cain, "Where is your brother Abel?" "I don't know," he replied.

> "Am I my brother's keeper?" The Lord said, "What have you done? Listen! Your brother's blood cries out to me from the ground. Now you are under a curse and driven from the ground, which opened its mouth to receive your brother's blood from your hand."
>
> —Genesis 4:6–11

God doesn't put curses or sickness on people, but Satan does. God is perfect love. He only wants what's best. It is never His will for His children to hurt or have any sickness, and any time any human says that it's God's will for someone to be sick or for a women to have a miscarriage or it's God's will for anything that brings death or destruction, then they obviously don't know God or His Word very well. John 10:10 (KJV) says, "The thief cometh not, but for to steal, and to kill, and to destroy: I am come that they might have life, and that they might have it more abundantly." God knows that every time we sin it opens up a doorway for Satan to come into our lives, to steal from us, try to kill us, and to destroy us and all that we have. But Jesus came so that He could protect us and so that we could have a life without sickness and a life of abundance—and not just when we die, but right now. Jesus is the same yesterday, today, and forever (Heb. 13:8). If He healed then, He will heal now and forever. God is not a respecter of persons (Acts 10:34). He loves all people the same. If He heals one, He will heal all. All He asks is for us to trust in Him, know Him, and for us to believe that He can and wants to heal.

Because God knew that a bad heart would lead to sin and that as soon as Cain sinned Satan would be at his door ready to wreak havoc on his life, God wanted to warn him, just as He oftentimes warns us. But because Cain didn't obey God—he sinned and killed his brother—Satan was able to put a curse on Cain's life. Cain ended up becoming a wanderer for the rest of his life. (See Genesis 4:11–16.)

> This is the message you heard from the beginning: We should love one another. Do not be like Cain, who belonged to the evil one and murdered his brother. And why did he murder him? Because his own actions were evil and his brother's were righteous. Do not be surprised, my brothers and sisters, if the world hates you. We know that we have passed from death to life, because we love each other. Anyone who does not love remains in death. Anyone who hates a brother or sister is a murderer, and you know that no murderer has eternal life residing in him. This is how we know what love is: Jesus Christ laid down his life for us. And we ought to lay down our lives for our brothers and sisters. If anyone has material possessions and sees a brother or sister in need but has no pity on them, how can the love of God be in that person? Dear children, let us not love with words or speech but with actions and in truth. This is how we know that we belong to the truth and how we set our hearts at rest in his presence: If our hearts condemn us, we know that God is greater than our hearts, and he knows everything. Dear friends, if our hearts do not condemn us, we have confidence before God and receive from him anything we ask, because we keep his commands and do what pleases him.
>
> —1 John 3:11–22

First Corinthians 13:13 (KJV) says, "And now abideth faith, hope, charity, these three; but the greatest of these is charity." In this verse the word *charity* means "an unbiased love that does not esteem one person or side more than another." So the three most important qualities that God wants us to have are: faith, hope, and an unbiased love toward one another. Love is the very foundation to life. God is perfect love, and He wants us not only to love for the sake of others but for ourselves. To love is to be free. This was another one of Cain's problems. He didn't love his brother. Cain was jealous of Abel. One of the meanings to the word *jealous* is "envious: feeling bitter and unhappy because of another's advantages, possessions, or blessings." The Bible says that if we do not love, we remain in death and can never have true happiness. In fact, the Bible actually says that if we don't love we can't have eternal life (1 John 3:15). Christ is the perfect example of God's perfect love. He laid down His life for us to pay our debt. So, God wants us to lay down our lives for one another in the sense that we love with actions.

> And now I will show you the most excellent way. If I speak in the tongues of men and of angels, but have not love, I am only a resounding gong or a clanging cymbal. If I have the gift of prophecy and can fathom all mysteries and all knowledge, and if I have a faith that can move mountains, but have not love, I am nothing. If I give all I possess to the poor and surrender my body to the flames, but have not love, I gain nothing.
>
> —1 Corinthians 12:31–13:1–3

No matter what gifts we have or where we are in life, if we do not love, we are nothing and we gain nothing!

What exactly is love? How is it defined? According to 1 Corinthians 13:4–8:

> Love is patient, love is kind. It does not envy, it does not boast, it is not proud. It is not rude, it is not self-seeking, it is not easily angered, it keeps no record of wrongs. Love does not delight in evil but rejoices with the truth. It always protects, always trusts, always hopes, always perseveres. Love never fails. But where there are prophecies, they will cease; where there are tongues, they will be stilled; where there is knowledge, it will pass away.

This verse is overused to the point that I think people don't really read it and let the truth flow over them. It's the same as the Lord's Prayer and other verses that are commonplace. They are used a lot because they are really wonderful, but when we constantly see something over and over again we stop really looking at the truth in them.

God is love, and this is the kind of love that He loves us with. God is patient, enduring our nonsense and not quickly angered. He is kind and compassionate, always wanting to help us. He's never arrogant or rude. He isn't selfish but loves us with an unconditional love, which is a love without condition or limitation. He keeps no record of wrong, and when we come to Him asking Him for forgiveness He is quick not only to forgive but to throw our sins as far as the east is from the west, remembering them no more. God is truth, and in Him there is no lie. His love will set us free from every bondage that the enemy has ever tried to put us in. His love will never fail us or let us down. Everything on this earth will one day pass away, but He and His love will remain.

God wants us to love like this. He wants us to endure others, being patient with them, even when it's hard. He wants us to be kind and compassionate. He wants us humble and not looking at ourselves as better than anyone. He wants us to love with an unselfish love, putting others first. And God wants us to be slow to anger, quickly forgiving everyone who has ever wronged us, as God in heaven forgives us. This at times seems impossible. I, for one, know how hard it is to love. I'm sure there have been a lot of people who have had a hard time loving me, but it's imperative that we obey God in this.

One of my favorite stories, that I believe truly shows great love and forgiveness is the story of Corrie ten Boom. Corrie (Cornelia) ten Boom was born in Holland in 1892. Corrie and her family were Christians and together they helped countless Jews escape the Nazi Holocaust during World War II. Because of their endeavors, in 1944, they were all arrested. Her father was taken to Scheveningen Prison, where ten days later he died. The rest of her family was released, but Corrie and her sister Betsie were both taken to Ravensbruck concentration camp, where Betsie later died.

After surviving the hostilities of the concentration camp, Corrie felt it was her calling to tell others about God's love and forgiveness. With God's provisions, she traveled the world over telling others the Good News about how God's love can overcome, heal, and restore.

In 1947, Corrie was in a church in Munich when she saw him, a former S.S. man who had stood guard at the shower room door at the Ravensbruck concentration camp. She had come from Holland to defeated Germany with a message that God forgives. It was a truth that the people of Germany needed most to hear at that time in history.

I can envision all of those faces staring up at her, each one with their own unique story of heartache and despair. Faces with eyes that had seen war ravage their nation; a war that had taken family members, friends, and people within their community forever. Infantrymen filled their street, warplanes filled the skies, sounds and smells filled the air that few generations could imagine. She was speaking to a broken and needy people.

Could you imagine what it would be like to possibly meet one of your captors? To be in a situation where you were brought face to face with someone who had treated you so inhumanly, someone who had been a part of the death of someone you loved and treasured as much as Corrie loved and treasured her sister, Betsie? This is exactly what happened at this particular meeting.

Corrie was finishing up her meeting and people were getting up and quietly leaving, and a man was making his way forward.

The vision of the past came rushing back to her, taking her to rooms with unforgiving lights and piles of lady's clothes and shoes, the outline of her frail sister's body walking past her, and feeling the shame of walking naked past this very man. This man had been one of the guards—one of the cruelest guards. He was working his way through the crowd towards her, and her once calm, sure thoughts started racing, trying to grasp what was taking place, then he was before her, hand stretched out. Once a tool that had been used against many, was now lifted in a cordial manner greeting her as a real person.

With his hand still held out, he started saying that he was a guard where she had been held prisoner. He continued on saying that he had come to be a Christian, and that he knew that he had been forgiven. When he had finished his story, His hand outstretched, he then asked her for forgiveness. Can you imagine such a thing, how could she find it within herself to forgive such a man? His words ringing within her, "will you forgive me?"

> And I, who had spoken so glibly of forgiveness, fumbled with my hands at my side.
>
> I stood there—I whose sins had again and again needed to be forgiven-and could not forgive. Betsie had died in that place-could he erase her slow terrible death simply for the asking?
>
> It could not have been many seconds that he stood there, hand held out, but to me it seemed hours as I wrestled with the most difficult thing I had ever had to do.
>
> For I had to do it—I knew that. The message that God forgives has a prior condition: that we forgive those who have injured us (Mark 11:25–26).
>
> And still I stood there with the coldness clutching my heart. But forgiveness is not an emotion—I knew that too. Forgiveness is an act of the will. "Jesus, help me!" I prayed. "I can lift my hand, I can do that much. You supply the feeling."[2]
>
> And so woodenly, mechanically, I thrust my hand into the one outstretched to me. And as I took his hand the most incredible thing happened. From my shoulder along my arm and through my hand a current seemed to pass from

> me to him, while into my heart sprang a love for this stranger that almost overwhelmed me. [3]
>
> "I forgive you, brother!" I cried. "With all my heart!"
>
> For a long moment we grasped each other's hands, the former guard and the former prisoner. I had never known God's love so intensely as I did then. But even so, I realized it was not my love. I had tried, and did not have the power. It was the love of the Holy Spirit.[4]

Truly, what an amazing story of love and forgiveness! And like Corrie ten Boom said, "Forgiveness is not an emotion…Forgiveness is an act of the will, and the will can function regardless of the temperature of the heart." That is true with everything that God asks us to do by faith. Faith is not an emotion but a choice. Love is not an emotion but a choice. And forgiveness is not an emotion but a choice. God doesn't say He wants us to feel forgiveness or feel faith or feel love, He just tells us to *do*! Everything is a choice.

Second Corinthians 5:7 says, "For we walk by faith, not by sight." What we see and feel are usually not going to go along with what God wants us to do. Abel probably felt tempted to not bring God his best. We all fall short, and we oftentimes have thoughts and temptations go through our hearts that aren't right, but it's not the temptation that's the sin; it's what we do in light of that temptation that is either righteous or a sin. Even Jesus was tempted (Luke 4:1–14), but in His temptations He did not sin (2 Cor. 5:21).

Abel decided to make a choice to bring God his best, and because of that the writer of Hebrews says in Hebrews 11:4 (KJV), "By faith Abel offered unto God a more excellent sacrifice than Cain, by which he obtained witness that he was righteous, God testifying of his gifts: and by it he being dead yet speaketh." So even though Abel died doing what was right, his actions still speak to us today. His actions say to us to walk by faith, trust God, and give God our very best.

Because of Cain's greed and his lack of love for his brother he chose to harbor anger, resentment, jealousy, and hatred. God warned him to what was in his heart, but instead of choosing the righteous path he chose instead to sin, and in his anger, resentment, jealousy, and hatred he killed his brother. Not giving God our best isn't a sin, but a poor heart condition that if left unchecked can cause us not only to sin but possibly be cursed for the duration of our lives. Give God your best in everything!

4

ELIJAH VS. AHAB

Obey God, Never Compromising

You need to persevere so that when you have done the will of God, you will receive what he has promised. For, "In just a little while, he who is coming will come and will not delay." And, "But my righteous one will live by faith. And I take no pleasure in the one who shrinks back." But we do not belong to those who shrink back and are destroyed, but to those who have faith and are saved.

—HEBREWS 10:36–39

GOD HAS CONTINUED to use many people since the days of the Bible. There have been many men and women who have done great things for God and have been willing, trustworthy vessels for the sake of the gospel. I really enjoy hearing about the great things God has done through these people. It amazes me how God can take and use imperfect vessels and raise the dead, heal the sick, bring sight to the blind, hearing to the deaf, and do many other astounding miracles.

One of those people who God used greatly was John

G. Lake. John G. Lake was born in 1870. People say that He was a man of great compassion who stood for the truth no matter what the consequence and that he set his sights high, refusing to compromise. One of the things that John G. Lake said was, "If I were to give you a watchword, it would be 'No compromise,' fight or no fight, discussion or no discussion. Principle is better than unity, and the ultimate end of principle will be oneness."[1]

John G. Lake was an amazing man of God who God used to heal numerous people and bring many to the Lord. The stories about the healings that took place under his ministry are so wonderful. He had a healing room where the sick would go to get healed. The Healing Room was located in Washington State, and in the first five years that it was open, it was reported that one hundred thousand people were healed.[2] One day a lady went to the Healing Room for prayer because she was sick. The men that prayed over her prayed that God would make her whole. Three months later she returned to the Healing Room a little disturbed; she was pregnant. Now, that doesn't seem odd to you or me, but to her it was really amazing, because she had previously had a complete and total hysterectomy. God not only healed her of her sickness, but He literally made her whole.[3]

Despite the great move of God in John G. Lake's ministry there was also a lot of jealousy and opposition. Some of the people were so set against him and his ministry that they wrote letters to the United States (his main ministry was in Africa) telling people that he was misusing finances, which later proved false. But because of these false accusations the little money that had been sent to his ministry before dwindled down to nothing. He had one hundred and twenty-five men out on the mission field at one time, and the money situation became so bad that John G. Lake wasn't able to send the people any money to sustain them. So, John G. Lake and many of the ministers sold their own personal belongings and clothes to bring the workers in off the field so that they could have a conference. At the conference the one hundred and twenty-five men made the decision to go back on the field to preach the gospel, saying, "We are going back to our fields. We are going back if we have to walk back. We are going back if we have to starve. We are going back if our wives die. We are going back if our children die. We are going back if we die ourselves. We have but one request. If we die, we want you [John G. Lake] to come and bury us."[4]

The next year John G. Lake buried twelve men, sixteen wives, and some of their children. John G. Lake said, "Do you know why God poured out His Spirit in South Africa like He did nowhere else in the world?... Friends, if you want to find out why the power of God came down from heaven like it never came down before, since the times of the apostles, there is your answer."[5]

These men, like Jesus' disciples, were willing to give up everything, including their lives, for the sake of the gospel. They were never willing to compromise but were always determined to stand strong until the end, and this was the reason that the Spirit of God could move in South Africa like He did.

God can only use people as much as they are willing to push through and be used. To compromise is to settle for less and to come to an agreement that is less than you originally wanted. When you set out on a journey for the Lord and times get tough, do you settle for less than the best? Do you think that it's not a big deal if you choose less? In not pushing through the obstacles in life and just settling you have not only compromised, but you have truly come to an agreement or settlement with Satan. Just like Revelation 3:15–16 says, it is better to be hot or cold, because if you are lukewarm, God will spit you out of His mouth. Like John G. Lake says, "Fight or no fight"[6]—don't do a little of both. Stick to what you say and want without compromise or settlement. The only way that God can truly use you is if you choose to go through life never compromising.

Daniel was willing to be thrown into a den of lions rather than bow down to anyone but God Almighty. Shadrach, Meshach, and Abednego were willing to be thrown into a blazing furnace instead of worship an image of gold. The Bible is filled with men and women who refused to compromise, and not only did their actions glorify God but in the end they were blessed.

Shadrach, Meshach, and Abednego, after disobeying the king and being thrown into a blazing furnace, not only didn't die because God supernaturally protected them, but God also gave them a place of recognition. King Nebuchadnezzar said:

> "Praise be to the God of Shadrach, Meshach and Abednego, who has sent his angel and rescued his servants! They trusted in him and defied the king's command and were willing to give up their lives rather than serve or worship any god except their own God. Therefore I decree that the people of any nation or language who say anything against the God of Shadrach, Meshach and Abednego be cut into pieces and their houses be turned into piles of rubble, for no

> other god can save in this way." Then the king promoted Shadrach, Meshach and Abednego in the province of Babylon.
>
> —Daniel 3:28–30

It would have been really easy for Shadrach, Meshach, and Abednego to compromise and say, "We will bow down with our bodies, but in our hearts we know that we are not truly worshiping this idol. We will continue to worship God but just pretend to do what the king asks so we can save our lives. Plus, if we die, then how will we ever be able to lead people to God?" You can visualize this argument as being very realistic. The only problem is, this is compromise, and compromise is never good in any circumstance.

We've all compromised in life. We've all done things that we knew were wrong because it either looked good to our flesh or because it was an easier path to take. But God wants us to be a people without compromise. He doesn't want us to be double minded and unstable in all we do (James 1:8).

> Ahab son of Omri did more evil in the eyes of the Lord than any of those before him. He not only considered it trivial to commit the sins of Jeroboam son of Nebat, but he also married Jezebel daughter of Ethbaal king of the Sidonians, and began to serve Baal and worship him. He set up an altar for Baal in the temple of Baal that he built in Samaria. Ahab also made an Asherah pole and did more to arouse the anger of the Lord, the God of Israel, than did all the kings of Israel before him
>
> —1 Kings 16:30–33

Ahab, like King Jeroboam, thought nothing of compromising his family, life, and kingship to do things his way. Both men were evil in the eyes of the Lord, showing no respect for God and disobeying Him at every turn.

To really understand Ahab we have to go back to King Solomon. King Solomon was a good king who loved God and wanted wisdom over wealth, and because of that God gave him both. The only problem was that Solomon, like his father, David, had a weak spot. That weakness was women. But unlike David, who learned his lesson and asked God for forgiveness for committing adultery with the wife of Uriah, Solomon let his weakness rule his life.

It says in 1 Kings 11:1–13 (KJV):

> But king Solomon loved many strange women, together with the daughter of Pharaoh, women of the Moabites, Ammonites, Edomites, Zidonians, and Hittites: Of the nations concerning which the LORD said unto the children of Israel, Ye shall not go in to them, neither shall they come in unto you: for surely they will turn away your heart after their gods: Solomon clave unto these in love. And he had seven hundred wives, princesses, and three hundred concubines: and his wives turned away his heart. For it came to pass, when Solomon was old, that his wives turned away his heart after other gods: and his heart was not perfect with the LORD his God, as was the heart of David his father. For Solomon went after Ashtoreth the goddess of the Zidonians, and after Milcom the abomination of the Ammonites. And Solomon did evil in the sight of the LORD, and went not fully after

> the LORD, as did David his father. Then did Solomon build an high place for Chemosh, the abomination of Moab, in the hill that is before Jerusalem, and for Molech, the abomination of the children of Ammon. And likewise did he for all his strange wives, which burnt incense and sacrificed unto their gods. And the LORD was angry with Solomon, because his heart was turned from the LORD God of Israel, which had appeared unto him twice, and had commanded him concerning this thing, that he should not go after other gods: but he kept not that which the LORD commanded. Wherefore the LORD said unto Solomon, Forasmuch as this is done of thee, and thou hast not kept my covenant and my statutes, which I have commanded thee, I will surely rend the kingdom from thee, and will give it to thy servant. Notwithstanding in thy days I will not do it for David thy father's sake: but I will rend it out of the hand of thy son. Howbeit I will not rend away all the kingdom; but will give one tribe to thy son for David my servant's sake, and for Jerusalem's sake which I have chosen.

Solomon loved his foreign wives more than he loved God, and because of that he was led astray by them and built high places for other gods. He was no longer fully devoted to God, and because of this God said He would tear the kingdom away from Solomon and give it to another. But, for the sake of David, He would not take Solomon's kingdom until he died. So, when Solomon died God took most of the kingdom from Solomon's son Rehoboam and gave it to Jeroboam.

Jeroboam was a man of standing and was a hard worker who did his work well. A prophet met Jeroboam on his way out of Jerusalem and told Jeroboam:

> For this is what the Lord, the God of Israel, says: "See, I am going to tear the kingdom out of Solomon's hand and give you ten tribes. But for the sake of my servant David and the city of Jerusalem, which I have chosen out of all the tribes of Israel, he will have one tribe. I will do this because they have forsaken me and worshiped Ashtoreth the goddess of the Sidonians, Chemosh the god of the Moabites, and Molek the god of the Ammonites, and have not walked in obedience to me, nor done what is right in my eyes, nor kept my decrees and laws as David, Solomon's father, did.... However, as for you, I will take you, and you will rule over all that your heart desires; you will be king over Israel. If you do whatever I command you and walk in obedience to me and do what is right in my eyes by obeying my decrees and commands, as David my servant did, I will be with you. I will build you a dynasty as enduring as the one I built for David and will give Israel to you."
>
> —1 Kings 11:31–33, 37–38

So, God was willing to allow Jeroboam to rule all that his heart desired and give him a lasting dynasty, which was a prominent and powerful family, and give him Israel. All he had to do was not compromise, doing whatever the Lord commanded him to do and walking in the ways of the Lord. But Jeroboam feared that his kingdom would be taken from him and given back to Rehoboam, so we read in 1 Kings 12:26–28, 31–32:

> Jeroboam thought to himself, "The kingdom will now likely revert to the house of David. If these people go up to offer sacrifices at the temple of the LORD in Jerusalem, they will again give their allegiance to their lord, Rehoboam king of Judah. They will kill me and return to King Rehoboam." After seeking advice, the king made two golden calves. He said to the people, "It is too much for you to go up to Jerusalem. Here are your gods, Israel, who brought you up out of Egypt"....Jeroboam built shrines on high places and appointed priests from all sorts of people, even though they were not Levites. He instituted a festival on the fifteenth day of the eighth month, like the festival held in Judah, and offered sacrifices on the altar. This he did in Bethel, sacrificing to the calves he had made. And at Bethel he also installed priests at the high places he had made.

Jeroboam made idols for the people. These idols were actually supposed to be God. He said, "Here are your gods, O Israel, who brought you up out of Egypt." He even made a holiday for these idols. There are a lot of people of the Christian faith—now, when I say "Christian faith" I don't necessarily mean that they are saved but that they base some of their lives around what the Old and New Testaments say—who because they can't see God with their eyes think nothing of taking objects and praying to them and believe that these objects can help them in bad situations. Sometimes it may even be a picture of what they think Jesus looked like. They actually think that when they pray to a cross or a picture they are praying to God. But God is not an object to be worshiped. God didn't want His people bowing down to objects, even if they believed in their hearts that they were actually worshiping God.

I don't think Jeroboam intended to be a bad king. My husband knew a guy who would say, "Good intentions pave the road to hell." What an incredibly true statement. I believe that Jeroboam had good intentions, but because of fear, greed, and many other sins in his life he compromised and took less than what God wanted for him. In turn Jeroboam ended up being not only a poor king, but he led many people astray.

Jeroboam had heard what God promised, but over time he started to let fear in. That fear made him not trust God, and because of his greed for his position as king he decided that it would be easier if he took matters into his own hands. How many times in life, because of fear or some other hidden sin, do we do the same thing? God gives us a promise, but in waiting for that promise to come forth we start to listen to Satan and our flesh—and all of a sudden we are taking matters into our own hands.

Abraham and Sarah did the same thing with the promise of Isaac (Gen. 15:1–18:15). God promised to give them a child, but doubt came into play. They tried to take things into their own hands, and what a mess that created. When we stop trusting God and take matters into our own hands we choose an inferior way, a compromise. This is what Jeroboam did.

The Bible says that King Ahab was even worse than King Jeroboam and even did more to provoke the Lord to anger than anyone. Ahab's opposite or counterpart was the prophet Elijah. Elijah was a great man of faith. He trusted in God and didn't compromise. God was able to use Elijah in some incredible situations because of his trustworthy obedience.

> Now Elijah the Tishbite, from Tishbe in Gilead, said to Ahab, "As the LORD, the God of Israel, lives, whom I serve, there will be neither dew nor rain in the next few years except at my word."
>
> —1 KINGS 17:1

Because of the lack of rain, for three years there was a great famine in the land. During those three years the Lord told Elijah to hide from Ahab and his evil wife, Jezebel. Jezebel had been killing all of the Lord's prophets, but a devout believer in God named Obadiah had taken a hundred prophets and hidden them in two different caves.

God told Elijah after three years to go and present himself to King Ahab, and He would send rain on the land. So Elijah went to present himself to Ahab.

> When he saw Elijah, he said to him, "Is that you, you troubler of Israel?" "I have not made trouble for Israel," Elijah replied. "But you and your father's family have. You have abandoned the LORD's commands and have followed the Baals. Now summon the people from all over Israel to meet me on Mount Carmel. And bring the

> four hundred and fifty prophets of Baal and the four hundred prophets of Asherah, who eat at Jezebel's table." So Ahab sent word throughout all Israel and assembled the prophets on Mount Carmel. Elijah went before the people and said, "How long will you waver between two opinions? If the Lord is God, follow him; but if Baal is God, follow him." But the people said nothing. Then Elijah said to them, "I am the only one of the Lord's prophets left, but Baal has four hundred and fifty prophets."
>
> —1 Kings 18:17–22

So Elijah told the prophets to get two bulls; they could choose one, and Elijah would have the other. So the prophets of Baal took their pick of bulls and cut the bull up into pieces and put it on the altar of wood. Then Elijah told them to call on their god, and if their god answered them by fire, then he was the greater god. So the prophets of Baal thought this sounded good.

> Then they called on the name of Baal from morning till noon. "Baal, answer us!" they shouted. But there was no response; no one answered. And they danced around the altar they had made. At noon Elijah began to taunt them. "Shout louder!" he said. "Surely he is a god! Perhaps he is deep in thought, or busy, or traveling. Maybe he is sleeping and must be awakened." So they shouted louder and slashed themselves with swords and spears, as was their custom, until their blood flowed. Midday passed, and they continued their frantic prophesying until the time for the evening sacrifice.

> But there was no response, no one answered, no one paid attention.
>
> —1 Kings 18:26–29

So then Elijah told the people to come to him, and he repaired the altar of the Lord, which was in ruins. Elijah took twelve stones, one for each of the tribes of Judah, and built an altar in the name of the Lord. Then he dug a trench around the altar. He arranged the wood, cut the bull into pieces and laid it on the wood.

> Then he said to them, "Fill four large jars with water and pour it on the offering and on the wood. Do it again," he said, and they did it again. "Do it a third time," he ordered, and they did it the third time. The water ran down around the altar and even filled the trench. At the time of sacrifice, the prophet Elijah stepped forward and prayed: "Lord, the God of Abraham, Isaac and Israel, let it be known today that you are God in Israel and that I am your servant and have done all these things at your command. Answer me, Lord, answer me, so these people will know that you, Lord, are God, and that you are turning their hearts back again." Then the fire of the Lord fell and burned up the sacrifice, the wood, the stones and the soil, and also licked up the water in the trench. When all the people saw this, they fell prostrate and cried, "The Lord—he is God! The Lord—he is God!" Then Elijah commanded them, "Seize the prophets of Baal. Don't let anyone get away!" They seized them, and Elijah had them brought down to the Kishon Valley and slaughtered there. And Elijah

> said to Ahab, "Go, eat and drink, for there is the sound of a heavy rain."
>
> —1 Kings 18:33–41

Ahab had tried to put the blame for the famine on Elijah, when it was really his and the people's sin that had caused the famine. When we blame others for our problems, we are trying to take the easy way out. If it's another person's problem, then we never have to own up to it and go through the work to fix ourselves. The thing about Ahab was that he was a weak man who took the counsel of man over God. He listened and obeyed his evil wife and the prophets of a god with no power rather than bow down and make his life right with God. He wanted to take the easier road. I'm sure the reason that Ahab and Jezebel were killing off all of the Lord's prophets was because the prophets were righteous and bringing words from the Lord that convicted Ahab. But instead of dealing with his issues he would rather kill the one bringing conviction. I am convinced the prophets of Baal told him exactly what his itching ears wanted to hear.

The second thing we notice after Ahab tries to blame Elijah for his problems is that Elijah gets the people in one place and asks them to choose. He tells them that they can't serve both Baal and God: "How long will you waiver between two opinions? If the Lord is God follow him; but if Baal is God, follow him" (1 Kings 18:21). Elijah told the people to compromise no longer but to choose once and for all who they would serve and to quit riding the fence—either God or Baal, not both!

After God's great show of power on Mount Carmel, the Bible says in 1 Kings 19:1–2 (KJV), "And Ahab told

Jezebel all that Elijah had done, and withal how he had slain all the prophets with the sword. Then Jezebel sent a messenger unto Elijah, saying, So let the gods do to me, and more also, if I make not thy life as the life of one of them by to morrow about this time." So Elijah ran for his life.

This whole time prophets of God were dying under the hands of King Ahab and Jezebel, all because they wouldn't compromise and tell Ahab and Jezebel what they wanted to hear. Elijah was one of these uncompromising prophets. I'm sure it was a scary thing to go before Ahab after three years of no rain when Elijah knew that Ahab was going to blame him for the lack of rain, but Elijah obeyed God. Because of his obedience, God was able to do a great work, which included turning the hearts of the people back to Him. When we don't compromise, God can use us greatly.

So, Elijah was on the run from Jezebel. He finally made it to Horeb, the mountain of God, where he found a cave to spend the night in.

> And the word of the LORD came to him: "What are you doing here, Elijah?" He replied, "I have been very zealous for the LORD God Almighty. The Israelites have rejected your covenant, torn down your altars, and put your prophets to death with the sword. I am the only one left, and now they are trying to kill me too." The LORD said, "Go out and stand on the mountain in the presence of the LORD, for the LORD is about to pass by." Then a great and powerful wind tore the mountains apart and shattered the rocks before the LORD, but the LORD was not in the wind. After the wind there was an earthquake,

> but the LORD was not in the earthquake. After the earthquake came a fire, but the LORD was not in the fire. And after the fire came a gentle whisper.
>
> —1 KINGS 19:9–12

This is an amazing piece of scripture, and yet I feel like I have such a small revelation of what it means. I think that Elijah had always known God as extremely powerful, like how the fire of the Lord fell on Mount Carmel, burning up everything—the bull, the dirt, the water, and even the rocks—showing an amazing display of His great power. And I think that Elijah had also known God to be very violent, fierce, and intense. But God has two sides. When Elijah is at his weakest, God comes along and tells Elijah that He will pass by, so then this powerful wind, which tears the mountain apart, passes by. Then an earthquake. And after the earthquake, there is a fire, and God is not in any of these. Instead, He is in a gentle whisper, or like the King James Version of the Bible says, "A still small voice." God is powerful and intense, but He is also soft and gentle. Elijah really needed this at this time in his life. He needed God's love and compassion, and God gave it.

Then God gives him hope. God tells Elijah to go back the way he came and go into the Desert of Damascus. When he gets there, there will be a man to anoint as king over Israel, a man named Elisha to succeed him as prophet, and God also tells Elijah he is not the only one left but that He has reserved seven thousand people whose knees have not bowed down to Baal and whose mouths have not kissed him.

How incredible for Elijah to hear. He was on his last

straw, and God comes along showing him love and compassion and tells him that He has it all taken care of. All is good in the hands of the Lord. We all go through times in our lives when we've had enough. We are hurt, sad, lonely, and we just want to be done. But not only does God have it all taken care of, but His presence is always there gently leading us, holding us, and making everything better like the great Daddy He is.

God doesn't want us to compromise and take less than what He has for us. He wants us to follow Him no matter what the cost, and when we do our lives will never be the same.

> But he that endureth to the end shall be saved.
>
> —MATTHEW 10:22, KJV

5

JOSHUA AND CALEB VS. THE TEN

Fear the Lord, Showing Him Great Respect and Admiration

By those who come near Me I must be regarded as holy; and before all the people I must be glorified.

—LEVITICUS 10:3, NKJV

There is a mine for silver and a place where gold is refined. Iron is taken from the earth, and copper is smelted from ore. Mortals put an end to the darkness; they search out the farthest recesses for ore in the blackest darkness. Far from human dwellings they cut a shaft, in places untouched by human feet; far from other people they dangle and sway. The earth, from which food comes, is transformed below as by fire; lapis lazuli comes from its rocks, and its dust contains nuggets of gold. No bird of prey knows that hidden path, no falcon's eye has seen it. Proud beasts do not set foot on it, and no lion prowls there. People assault the flinty rock with their hands and lay bare the roots of the mountains. They tunnel through the rock;

their eyes see all its treasures. They search the sources of the rivers and bring hidden things to light. But where can wisdom be found? Where does understanding dwell? No mortal comprehends its worth; it cannot be found in the land of the living. The deep says, "It is not in me"; the sea says, "It is not with me." It cannot be bought with the finest gold, nor can its price be weighed out in silver. It cannot be bought with the gold of Ophir, with precious onyx or lapis lazuli. Neither gold nor crystal can compare with it, nor can it be had for jewels of gold. Coral and jasper are not worthy of mention; the price of wisdom is beyond rubies. The topaz of Cush cannot compare with it; it cannot be bought with pure gold. Where then does wisdom come from? Where does understanding dwell? It is hidden from the eyes of every living thing, concealed even from the birds in the sky. Destruction and Death say, "Only a rumor of it has reached our ears." God understands the way to it and he alone knows where it dwells, for he views the ends of the earth and sees everything under the heavens. When he established the force of the wind and measured out the waters, when he made a decree for the rain and a path for the thunderstorm, then he looked at wisdom and appraised it; he confirmed it and tested it. And he said to the human race, "The fear of the Lord—that is wisdom, and to shun evil is understanding."

—Job 28:1–28

Wisdom can't be found. Men can't comprehend wisdom or its worth. Some people spend their whole lives searching for vast riches. They toil, spending exhausting hours searching to bring hidden things to light. But wisdom can't be bought with the finest gold. Its price can't be weighed in silver. Wisdom can't be bought with any precious stone, and nothing compares with it or its worth. So what is wisdom? God says, "The fear of the Lord—that is wisdom, and to shun evil is understanding" (Job 28:28).

Wisdom doesn't come with age. It says in Job 32:7–9, "I thought, 'Age should speak; advanced years should teach wisdom.' But it is the spirit in a person, the breath of the Almighty, that gives them understanding. It is not only the old who are wise, not only the aged who understand what is right."

A man of God named John Bevere wrote a wonderful book called *The Fear of the Lord*. In the first chapter of the book God really explains through John Bevere what it is to fear God.

It was 1997 and John was in Brazil speaking at a national conference. The first city he spoke at was the capital city of Brasilia. He said that the auditorium, which held approximately four thousand people, was full, and the people were singing high-intensity praise songs. Yet he quickly noted that there was a complete absence of the Lord's presence. So he inquired of the Lord to why there was an absence of His presence, and while he was waiting for the Lord to answer him he took notice of what was happening around the auditorium. He said there were people looking about, and many looked bored. People had their hands in their pockets or hanging heavily about their sides, as if casually waiting for a show to begin. Many people were going in and out of the auditorium and talking to one another.

John Bevere said that he was very grieved, because this wasn't an outreach but a believer's meeting. Most of the people in the crowd were Christians! He thought that maybe once the meeting began people would enter into a true reverence of God, and then surely the atmosphere would change. But as soon as the service began and the people were told to have a seat, not only did the people not change, but they continued on in casual conversation. John said, "One leader took the microphone to exhort the people, yet the people talked on."[1] Then they read from the Bible and taught, but the entire time there was a dull rumble of many voices speaking and people moving about, paying no attention to the speaker. He said that in frustration he turned to his Brazilian interpreter and asked if this was normal. The interpreter said that sometimes they had to actually ask the people to please pay attention.

The Spirit of God spoke to John Bevere and told him to directly confront this issue. When it was his turn to speak he got up on the stage and stood there looking at the crowd. He decided not to say anything until he had everyone's full attention. After about a minute the people began to fall silent because they realized that there was nothing happening on the platform.

John Bevere didn't introduce himself; instead, he asked the crowd how they would like it if while they spoke to someone they were ignored the entire time, or if while they spoke to someone the other person carried on a conversation with the person next to them. Or, how would they like it if while they were talking to someone that person's eyes roamed with disinterest and disrespect? He paused and answered his own question by saying that they wouldn't like it. He then questioned, "What if every time you rang the doorbell to visit a neighbor's house you were greeted with a careless attitude and monotone sigh. 'Oh, it's you again; come on in'?" He paused then added, "You wouldn't visit them anymore, would you?"[2]

He asked the people if they really thought that the King of kings and the Lord of lords was really going to come to a place where He was not given due honor and reverence. He then told the people what he saw when he walked into the building and how when God's Word was read the people esteemed it lightly. Then John read to them what God requires of those who come near Him: "By those who come near Me I must be regarded as holy; And before all the people I must be glorified" (Lev. 10:3, NKJV). For the next hour and a half John preached the message that God burned into his heart.

For that hour and a half John said that while he preached you could have heard a pin drop between his words, it was so quiet. After he preached, he asked that everyone close their eyes, and he gave a pointed and brief call for repentance. Without any hesitation seventy-five percent of the people rose to their feet and repented. Immediately the presence of the Lord filled the auditorium, and sobs and cries could be heard from the crowd. John said, "It was as if a wave of God's presence had swept through the building, bringing cleansing and refreshing."[3] After a few minutes God's presence subsided, but he told the people not to lose focus but to draw near to God and He would draw near to them (James 4:8). After that a few moments passed, and another wave of God's presence flooded the building.

The tears and crying intensified, and God's presence was more far reaching, as more people were touched. Again God's presence subsided, and he told them again not to lose focus.

The rest is really incredible and would be better if it was told from John Bevere's point of view.

> What I now write will in no way accurately represent what happened next. My words are too limited and God too awesome. Neither will I exaggerate, for that would also be irreverent. I interviewed three other leaders who were present to clarify and confirm what I now record.
>
> No sooner had the word "again" left my lips when the following happened. The only way I know how to describe it is to compare it to standing a hundred or so yards away from the end of a runway as a huge jet takes off right in front of you. This describes the roar of the wind that immediately blew through that auditorium. Almost simultaneously the people erupted in fervent and intense prayer, their voices rising and combining into almost a single shout.[4]

John Bevere said that the sound was so loud it overpowered the people's voices and lasted approximately two minutes.

> When it subsided, it left in its wake a praying, weeping people. The atmosphere was charged with holy reverence. The Lord's presence was very real and powerful. The awesome aftermath of His presence continued for fifteen to twenty minutes.[5]

John Bevere left the meeting shortly after, riding back to his hotel with his interpreter and a married couple who were also leaders. As they talked about all that had happened at the meeting one of the men had said that the security personnel and police outside the building reported hearing a mighty sound coming from inside the building. Outside of the building, there was no wind, and it was just another calm Brazilian evening. And the man's wife, with tears streaming down her face, said, "I saw waves of fire falling on the building and angels everywhere!"[6]

John could hardly believe his ears. Two months earlier he had heard this same description used by a minister while he preached on the fear of the Lord in North Carolina. John said, "I had preached on the fear of the Lord, and God's presence had fallen mightily on those assembled—more than a hundred little children wept profusely for an hour. A visiting minister told the pastor that she had seen waves of balls of fire falling on the building. This was also confirmed by three choir members."[7]

At the next meeting that he was scheduled to minister at before leaving for Rio de Janeiro, John said he went into the auditorium, and the entire atmosphere was different. He could sense a restored respect for the Lord. In the service, many were delivered and healed.

> Many who had been bound by bitterness and had harbored offences were set free. Where the Lord is reverenced, His presence manifests—and where his presence manifests, needs are met.[8]

> Oh how great is thy goodness, which thou hast laid up for them that fear thee; which thou hast wrought for them that trust in thee before the sons of men!
>
> —Psalm 31:19, KJV

God is so incredible, and we owe Him all of our reverence. If we can't give Him due respect, we will live our lives completely void of His presence. The Bible says in 2 Corinthians 3:17 (KJV), "Where the Spirit of the Lord is, there is liberty." There is truly nothing greater than the presence of God and the freedom therein.

The Book of Exodus tells the story of God's people, the Israelites.

> Now Joseph and all his brothers and all that generation died, but the Israelites were exceedingly fruitful; they multiplied greatly, increased in numbers and became so numerous that the land was filled with them. Then a new king, to whom Joseph meant nothing, came to power in Egypt. "Look," he said to his people, "the Israelites have become far too numerous for us. Come, we must deal shrewdly with them or they will become even more numerous and, if war breaks out, will join our enemies, fight against us and leave the country."
>
> —Exodus 1:6–10

After this the Egyptians put slave masters over the Israelites, oppressing them with forced labor. But the more they oppressed the Israelites, the more they multiplied. So the king of Egypt told the Hebrew midwives that if a woman had a male child she was to kill it. But the midwives didn't listen. The king summoned them and asked them why they had not listened, and the midwives said that the Hebrew women were different then the Egyptian women and delivered their babies so quickly that they had already had the babies by the time they got there. God was kind to the midwives, and the Israelites continued to multiply.

> And because the midwives feared God, he gave them families of their own.
>
> —Exodus 1:21

So the king of Egypt gave an order that all male Hebrew babies must be thrown into the Nile. We all know the story of Moses and how God spared him. Moses was chosen by God to lead the Israelites out of Egypt and lead them to the land that He had promised to them, which was the land of Canaan. After God had sent ten different plagues on the Egyptians, Pharaoh finally let the people go.

> When Pharaoh let the people go, God did not lead them on the road through the Philistine country, though that was shorter. For God said, "If they face war, they might change their minds and return to Egypt." So God led the people around by the desert road toward the Red Sea. The Israelites went up out of Egypt ready for battle.
>
> —Exodus 13:17–18

After the Israelites had left, Pharaoh changed his mind and went after them. He took six hundred of the best chariots, along with the rest of the chariots, with officers in all of them. When the Israelites saw the Egyptians coming after them they were terrified and cried out to God. Moses told the people:

> "Do not be afraid. Stand firm and you will see the deliverance the Lord will bring you today. The Egyptians you see today you will never see again. The Lord will fight for you; you need only to be still." Then the Lord said to Moses, "Why are you crying out to me? Tell the Israelites to move on. Raise your staff and stretch out your hand over the sea to divide the water so that the Israelites can go through the sea on dry ground"....Then the angel of God, who had been traveling in front of Israel's army, withdrew and went behind them. The pillar of cloud also moved from in front and stood behind them, coming between the armies of Egypt and Israel. Throughout the night the cloud brought darkness to the one side and light to the other side; so neither went near the other all night long. Then Moses stretched out his hand over the sea, and all that night the Lord drove the sea back with a strong east wind and turned it into dry land. The waters were divided.
>
> —Exodus 14:13–16, 19–21

Then the Israelites crossed the Red Sea, while the Egyptians continued to pursue them. As the Egyptians crossed the Red Sea God threw them into confusion, causing the wheels of their chariots to come off, so they had difficulty driving. The Egyptians soon realized that God was fighting for the Israelites and against Egypt, so they tried to flee. But God told Moses to stretch his hand over the sea again, and the sea went back to its place, swallowing the whole Egyptian army. Not one of them survived. When the Israelites saw the great power that the Lord displayed against the Egyptians, the people feared the Lord and put their trust in Him and in His servant, Moses.

The Lord continuously showed the Israelites one miracle after another, always providing for their every need. God protected and guided the Israelites in a pillar of cloud by day and a pillar of fire by night. The Lord gave them water and food (quail and manna) in the desert. But from the very beginning of the journey out of slavery and into freedom, the people complained. They complained that the work was too hard when God was sending plagues on the Egyptians, even though the Israelites were spared. They complained as they left Egypt that it would have been better to have served the Egyptians than to die in the desert. They complained about eating the same thing every day. The complaining and lack of trust never ceased. The people saw God's great might and awesome power, yet they found room to complain and show God disrespect over and over again.

God had the Israelites settle in the desert at the foot of Mount Sinai for about a year so that He could set up His covenant with them, giving them laws for living and worshiping. God gave the Israelites the Ten Commandments, priests, and a tabernacle to help them live godly lives. After about a year God decided that He wanted to give the Israelites the land that He had promised them, so He sent them out to explore the land that He wanted to give them.

> The LORD said to Moses, "Send some men to explore the land of Canaan, which I am giving to the Israelites. From each ancestral tribe send one of its leaders." So at the LORD's command Moses sent them out from the Desert of Paran. All of them were leaders of the Israelites. . . . When Moses sent them to explore Canaan, he said, "Go up through the Negev and on into the hill country. See what the land is like and whether the people who live there are strong or weak, few or many. What kind of land do they live in? Is it good or bad? What kind of towns do they live in? Are they unwalled or fortified? How is the soil? Is it fertile or poor? Are there trees in it or not? Do your best to bring back some of the fruit of the land." (It was the season for the first ripe grapes.) So they went up and explored the land from the Desert of Zin as far as Rehob, toward Lebo Hamath. They went up through the Negev and came to Hebron, where Ahiman, Sheshai and Talmai, the descendants of Anak, lived. (Hebron had been built seven years before Zoan in Egypt.) When they reached the Valley of Eshkol, they cut off a branch bearing a single cluster of grapes. Two of them carried it on a pole between them, along with some pomegranates and figs. That place was called the Valley of Eshkol because of the cluster of grapes the Israelites cut off there. At the end of forty days they returned from exploring the land. They came back to Moses and Aaron and the whole Israelite community at Kadesh in the Desert of

Paran. There they reported to them and to the whole assembly and showed them the fruit of the land. They gave Moses this account: "We went into the land to which you sent us, and it does flow with milk and honey! Here is its fruit. But the people who live there are powerful, and the cities are fortified and very large. We even saw descendants of Anak there. The Amalekites live in the Negev; the Hittites, Jebusites and Amorites live in the hill country; and the Canaanites live near the sea and along the Jordan." Then Caleb silenced the people before Moses and said, "We should go up and take possession of the land, for we can certainly do it." But the men who had gone up with him said, "We can't attack those people; they are stronger than we are." And they spread among the Israelites a bad report about the land they had explored. They said, "The land we explored devours those living in it. All the people we saw there are of great size. We saw the Nephilim there (the descendants of Anak come from the Nephilim). We seemed like grasshoppers in our own eyes, and we looked the same to them."

—Numbers 13:1–3, 17–33

That night all the members of the community raised their voices and wept aloud. All the Israelites grumbled against Moses and Aaron, and the whole assembly said to them, "If only we had died in Egypt! Or in this wilderness! Why is the Lord bringing us to this land only to let us fall by the sword? Our wives and children will be taken as plunder. Wouldn't it be better for us to go back to Egypt?" And they said to each other, "We should choose a leader and go back to Egypt." Then Moses and Aaron fell facedown in front of the whole Israelite assembly gathered there. Joshua son of Nun and Caleb son of Jephunneh, who were among those who had explored the land, tore their clothes and said to the entire Israelite assembly, "The land we passed through and explored is exceedingly good. If the Lord is pleased with us, he will lead us into that land, a land flowing with milk and honey, and will give it to us. Only do not rebel against the Lord. And do not be afraid of the people of the land, because we will devour them. Their protection is gone, but the Lord is with us. Do not be afraid of them." But the whole assembly talked about stoning them. Then the glory of the Lord appeared at the tent of meeting to all the Israelites. The Lord said to Moses, "How long will these people treat me with contempt? How long will they refuse to believe in me, in spite of all the signs I have performed among them? I will strike them down with a plague and destroy them, but I will make you into a nation greater and stronger than they." Moses said to the Lord, "Then the Egyptians will hear about it! By your power you brought these people up from among them. And they will tell the inhabitants of this land about it. They have already heard that you, Lord, are with these people and that you, Lord, have been seen face to face, that your cloud stays over them,and that you go before them in a pillar of cloud by day and a pillar of fire by night. If you put all these people to death, leaving none alive, the nations who have heard this report about you will say, 'The Lord was not able to bring these people into the land he promised them on oath, so he slaughtered them in the wilderness.' Now may the LORD's strength be displayed, just as you have declared: 'The LORD is slow to anger, abounding in love and forgiving sin and rebellion. Yet he does not leave the guilty unpunished; he punishes the children for the sin of the parents to the third and fourth generation.' In accordance with your great love, forgive the sin of these people, just as you have pardoned them from the time they left Egypt until now." The LORD replied, "I have forgiven them, as you asked. Nevertheless, as surely as I live and as surely as the glory of the LORD fills the whole earth, not one of those who saw my glory and the signs I performed in Egypt and in the wilderness but who disobeyed me and tested me ten times—not one of them will ever see the land I promised on oath to their ancestors. No one who has treated me with contempt will ever see it. But because my servant Caleb has a different spirit and follows me wholeheartedly, I will bring him into the land he went to, and his descendants will inherit it. Since the Amalekites and the Canaanites are living in the valleys, turn back tomorrow and set out toward the desert along the route to the Red Sea." The LORD said to Moses and Aaron: "How long will this wicked community grumble against me? I have heard the complaints of these grumbling Israelites. So tell them, 'As surely as I live, declares the LORD, I will do to you the very thing I heard you say: In this wilderness your bodies will fall—every one of you twenty years old or more who was counted in the census

> and who has grumbled against me. Not one of you will enter the land I swore with uplifted hand to make your home, except Caleb son of Jephunneh and Joshua son of Nun. As for your children that you said would be taken as plunder, I will bring them in to enjoy the land you have rejected. But as for you, your bodies will fall in this wilderness. Your children will be shepherds here for forty years, suffering for your unfaithfulness, until the last of your bodies lies in the wilderness. For forty years—one year for each of the forty days you explored the land—you will suffer for your sins and know what it is like to have me against you.' I, the Lord, have spoken, and I will surely do these things to this whole wicked community, which has banded together against me. They will meet their end in this wilderness; here they will die." So the men Moses had sent to explore the land, who returned and made the whole community grumble against him by spreading a bad report about it—these men who were responsible for spreading the bad report about the land were struck down and died of a plague before the Lord. Of the men who went to explore the land, only Joshua son of Nun and Caleb son of Jephunneh survived.
>
> —Numbers 14:1–38

When I read this, the word *contempt* really stuck out: "How long will these people treat me with contempt? How long will they refuse to believe in me, in spite of all the signs I have performed among them?" (Num. 14:11). And again the Lord said, "No one who has treated me with contempt will ever see it [meaning the Promise Land]" (Num. 14:23).

So, I wondered, what does *contempt* mean? And this is what I found: *Contempt* means "to have an attitude of utter disgust or hatred: a powerful feeling of dislike toward somebody or something considered to be worthless, inferior, or undeserving of respect." God knows our hearts, and according to Him these people had an attitude of utter disgust and hatred toward Him. They not only didn't trust Him and love Him for all that He did for them, but they considered Him to be worthless, inferior, and undeserving of their respect. God had brought them out of slavery, where they were forced to work all of their days for a cruel Pharaoh who was trying to kill off their children. Yet they actually thought that their lives in slavery were better than the freedom that God had given to them. God had provided for their every need, and yet they esteemed Him not.

God was now going to give these complaining, bitter, angry, hard, and weak people a land flowing with milk and honey. I've been to Israel, and one of my favorite places that I visited was the Promised Land. It is still to this day a land that is an oasis in the middle of a desert. It is truly beautiful with rivers and lush greenery, and God was willing to fight for them and give them the land. Yet, because of their disrespect for God and lack of trust, they lost out on what God had for them.

I'm sure that living in the desert wasn't easy. Nothing worth anything is ever easy. I think that when we are in bondage there is a certain comfort that we find in that bondage; that's why we often have a really hard time giving up sin. But God doesn't want us in bondage to anything. He wants us free. Obtaining freedom will always take work and will come with pain, just like dying to our flesh and what it wants and desires, but through it God wants us to have a good attitude. He wants us to look at Him and His greatness and thank Him for His bounty. He wants to take all of us to our Promise Land, so to speak. He wants us to be like Joshua and Caleb, who trusted in Him, knowing that He will continue to fight for us, always keeping our best interests in mind.

Fearing God is having a great reverence and respect for who He is. It's loving Him and admiring Him and His awesome power. God is so amazing; He loves us beyond anything we could ever imagine. He is the perfect Father, Friend, Husband, Love, and Savior any of us could ever want or need. People often try to find things in the world to fill the emptiness in their hearts but fail miserably because they are looking to the world to fill the void that only God can fill. Joshua and Caleb were the only two out of the twelve entrusted to go and spy out the land who believed in God and respected and trusted Him enough to keep His promise to them. They feared God, and the others didn't. Because of that they were the only two over the age of twenty who were allowed to enter into the Promised Land and occupy it.

God so desperately wants us to desire Him, trust Him, give our all to Him, never compromising for the things of the world. And He wants us to regard Him as holy, holding Him in high regard, and when we do, our lives will never be the same.

6

MARY VS. MARTHA

Live by Faith, Not by Works

Now to a laborer, his wages are not counted as a favor or a gift, but as an obligation (something owed to him). But to one who, not working [by the Law], trusts (believes fully) in Him Who justifies the ungodly, his faith is credited to him as righteousness (the standing acceptable to God).

—ROMANS 4:4–5, AMP

OVER THE LAST year I have been learning one of the greatest lessons in this life. I have always prayed that God would use me greatly, that I would be a trustworthy vessel that He would use to open blind eyes, open the ears of the deaf, heal the sick, raise the dead, bring good news to all, and proclaim freedom to the captives. I knew that I was not ready for this kind of venture before, but I have persistently cried out to God to mature me, make me ready, open my eyes, humble me, and make me more loving. I never really asked God to help me in my faith. I have always tried to take God at His Word, to believe that which He says in the Bible, and never to put God in a box. If God says,

"The one who is in you is greater than the one who is in the world" (1 John 4:4), I believe Him. If God says that He "wants all men to be saved and to come to a knowledge of the truth" (1 Tim. 2:4), then I believed Him then too. If God says He wants all healed and that healing has already been paid for, then I believe Him in this also. Everything in His Word I try to take at face value and believe that which He says. I never thought my faith needed work; only my personality, my flesh, and the many other things in my life.

I had flown through the writing of this book. God would put things on my heart and give me the words and the revelation on what to write, and I would write during every spare moment I had. Then in December of 2010 I really had nothing else to write. I knew that I wasn't finished, but I was stumped as to why I had flown through six chapters without any real block and now I had nothing. So I brought this to the Lord and asked Him, and I felt like I was supposed to write my next and possibly my last chapter on Mary and Martha. I thought, "Well, that should be easy." So I read and studied—and got nothing. So I prayed some more. And nothing.

Now my faith was really being tested. Satan brought all kinds of lies to my mind, and I started wondering if I had ever really heard God in any of this. Then I got a simple revelation that Mary represents faith and Martha represents works. Again, I was excited and thought, "Finally, I can write again," but every time I did, I got nothing. Little did I know that I would get little bits of revelation over the next year, and even now I feel like I will still be getting more over the next few months and years.

My first revelation came about a month later when

God blessed me and allowed me to be at the home birth of a wonderful friend. This was her first home birth, and the people who would be there would be her husband, a midwife, a friend of ours, and me. The birth went wonderfully. I got there, and she was consistently contracting, but her contractions weren't bad. So, her children and husband went to bed, and we stayed up and hung out. It was an enjoyable time. We went for a walk around midnight. It was a cold winter night; we live in northern Minnesota. The trees lined the road, making it seem even darker then it was. We walked a good half mile before we realized we'd better get back.

When we got back her contractions picked up, so she called our friend, the midwife, and woke up her husband. We started filling the water birth tub as her contractions hardened. The midwife got there a short time later, and she was definitely pretty far along at this point. We had been praying and believing for a quick, easy, safe, fearless, and somewhat painless delivery. The only real concern that she had—and voiced a few times—was that she wasn't looking forward to pushing. With her last baby the pushing was pretty intense, and so she said she didn't really want to push.

I have always known how important our words are when it comes to believing and having faith, but in this instance, God really showed me just how important that they are. At around three o'clock in the morning she was fully dilated. So, she tried to push, and nothing happened. There was really no verbal concern; we knew God was in control. Around morning she was so exhausted from trying to push off and on for five and a half hours, from going without any sleep or rest, and from being in labor for a long time that she was at the point of just being done. One thing to note: this was her fourth baby, and the other three babies all came within two pushes!

I prayed and felt like the Lord gave me some direction on what to do. I felt like I was supposed to command the baby to come, tell her husband that God had a word for him to say, and I felt like I was supposed to read the Word over her. Needless to say, I also learned a valuable lesson in obeying God. I argued with Him for a good hour or more, believing I was going mad, that I didn't really hear God, and that it wasn't my place to command her baby to come or tell her husband what to do. I have since then had to apologize for my disobedience to God and the fact that I think my disobedience kept her in labor longer then she should have been. I finally obeyed, but in my obedience I compromised. I decided to only do one of the things I felt God tell me to do; I read verses out loud.

Then when she was on her last straw, our friend spoke up and told her husband that she believed that God had a word for him to speak. I felt relieved and a little sad; I knew then that what I had been hearing was really from God, and because of my disobedience God chose to use someone else. My friend's husband didn't say anything for a moment, and then all of a sudden he spoke a very simple sentence, "God is in control." Within seconds she pushed that little baby boy out. Nothing had changed in five and a half hours; yet his words, spoken in faith and power, broke the lies of Satan. I learned just how incredibly important our words are. I now see more clearly how easy Satan's lies are to believe and that if we don't really believe God and His Word, we will fall for Satan's lies every time. But with God's Word of truth all of the lies and power of Satan will be broken. I went home realizing that I needed some work on my faith, and then I vowed that if I were ever put into a situation like that again I would be bold and obedient, even if someone thought I was ridiculous. I learned faith with actions changes situations!

My next chance for faith came in May 2011, when we had our sixth baby. I had my first three babies at the hospital with a nurse's midwife. I had them natural, without any drugs and/or medication. We did things our way and went home shortly after each of their births. We didn't let anyone take them from the room or do anything with them, and our experiences were wonderful. But the time came to have them at home. My first home birth went wonderfully. The midwife got there about a half an hour before our fourth baby boy was born. With the birth of our fifth baby we decided we wanted to do an unattended birth, without any midwife. We were going to trust God, not man.

But about a week before I had our first baby girl I allowed a spirit of fear in. While visiting with the midwife she accidentally made a comment that she didn't know if the baby was head down or not. I knew that she wasn't breech (upside down), but Satan started putting these little thoughts in my mind that maybe she was sideways. I tried to ignore the lies, but I never actually dealt with them with the Word of God. To make a long story short, she was perfect, healthy, and in a perfect position, but because of the little bit of fear that I had had the labor was extraordinarily intense.

I knew with my sixth baby that I did not want to have an intense birth but a wonderful experience, and my friend's birth really showed me how important our words are and how important it was to not have fear but only to trust in our wonderful Father. So I kept the fear out, and I trusted God. Because of it I had a wonderful birth. I went into labor at the perfect timing; the birth was wonderful, easy, and perfect in every way. Every time a contraction would hit I would start talking to God. I would tell Him how much I loved Him, how wonderful He was, and I would thank Him. And every time my contractions would lessen in pain. My contractions were seven minutes apart, and that never changed for the duration of my labor. Toward the end of the labor I actually heard God speaking to me in a still small voice. He would tell me that I was almost finished, He would encourage me, and He would tell me what to do with each contraction. I felt His presence very strongly, and His words brought so much comfort. He was the perfect coach.

Toward the end, my husband later said that he thought I had at least three hours of labor left just from watching me and seeing that my contractions were so far apart. During the last contractions I felt like God said that I had only two more to go and I would have the baby, and sure enough, in two contractions, I pushed out our sixth baby. God is great, and He is true to His Word.

Over the last year I have prayed for a revelation for faith. Knowing that the story of Mary and Martha was the next chapter I was to write, I kept studying that story. In looking up verses about faith versus works I came across Romans 4:4–5: "Now when a man works, his wages are not credited to him as a gift, but as an obligation. However, to the man who does not work but trusts

God who justifies the wicked, his faith is credited as righteousness."

Now when you have a job and you work, you are deserving of some sort of pay. Your employer would be wrong to give you the pay that you earned as though it were a gift, because it wasn't a gift but an obligation on his part. Faith is different. God gives us so many wonderful gifts, but we don't have to work for them because they are free. That work would be in vain. I feel like the church is in the place it is in because we keep trying to work for the gifts that have already been given. God doesn't want us to work for that which He has already given us. The whole point is that those gifts have already been paid for with the blood of His Son Jesus Christ, and when we try to work for that which He has already given to us and has already paid for it is really belittling that which Jesus did on the cross.

When I read this verse it was like a light went on. I realized that faith is simple, just believing and receiving, and that's it! We want to make everything work. When we're sick the Bible tells us that Jesus bought our healing on the cross. It's ours, and all we have to do is have faith, believe it is ours, and it is. But instead of keeping it simple and taking God at His Word and believing Him we try to do, do, do! We try to become better, more perfect. We try to please God and make sure that we don't do this or don't do that, we watch what we eat—but when will we ever be perfect enough to receive anything from our perfect God and Creator?

Now, don't get me wrong. I believe wholeheartedly in keeping our heart right and pure before God, but not because we are trying to get and earn things from Him.

> As Jesus and his disciples were on their way, he came to a village where a woman named Martha opened her home to him. She had a sister called Mary, who sat at the Lord's feet listening to what he said. But Martha was distracted by all the preparations that had to be made. She came to him and asked, "Lord, don't you care that my sister has left me to do the work by myself? Tell her to help me!" "Martha, Martha," the Lord answered, "you are worried and upset about many things, but few things are needed—or indeed only one. Mary has chosen what is better, and it will not be taken away from her."
>
> —Luke 10:38–42

How amazing is this story? You have two people once again, and one does what is right in the eyes of the Lord and the other does what is wrong. But in our world, it would be reversed. We would look at Martha and think that she was a hard worker, that she was carrying the weight of the family and taking care of all of the problems and the people. We would be proud of her and think that what she was doing was not only right but good. And then you have Mary, who is being irresponsible and is selfish in not helping her sister but instead is sitting, doing nothing. We would be irritated at her and her lack of work. But God saw things very differently. He saw a woman who was carrying the weight, but a weight that wasn't hers to bear. He saw a woman who was worried and upset about many things. But He says, "Don't worry about anything; instead, pray about everything. Tell God what you need, and thank him for all he has done" (Phil. 4:6, NLT).

He also saw a woman who was also distracted by

many things. The word *distracted* has two meanings: "showing a lack of concentration and...so worried or upset as to be unable to think clearly or act sensibly."

Then you have Mary, who chose what was better. She sat at the feet of the Maker without a thought or care or distraction in the world and loved Him.

God wants us to live by faith and faith alone. What is faith?

> Now faith is being sure of what we hope for and certain of what we do not see.
>
> —HEBREWS 11:1, NIV (1984)

God wants us to live by those things that we hope for, and He wants us to be certain about the things He has promised us. The word *certain* means "without doubt: having no doubts about something, inevitable: guaranteed to happen." He wants us to know Him, His personality, and His promises so well that we believe all that He tells us so that we know without any doubt that what He promises us is inevitable, unavoidable, and guaranteed to happen. God commands us that we must "live by faith, not by sight" (2 Cor. 5:7).

I am passionate about healing. I believe that in this day and age healing is one of those gifts and promises that we try too hard to work for instead of just receiving. Healing is a promise that is often difficult for us to really live out in our lives. It's a simple promise in that when Jesus died on the cross He not only died for our sins, so that we may have eternal life with Him, but He also died so that while we were on this earth we might live a life free from sickness and disease. God promises us healing, both emotionally and physically. But healing is difficult, because we can so easily see and feel sickness and disease and because most people believe that what the medical experts say is truth. What about God? Is what He says truth, or is it a lie? They cannot both be right. Either healing is ours or it's not. Is not God the same yesterday, today, and forever (Heb. 13:8)? If Jesus healed while He was on this earth, does He not still heal today—and forever? What it really comes down to is whether we truly believe that God is who He says He is or not.

God wants desperately for us to know Him and His promises, and He wants His people to live lives free from sickness and disease. He wants His people to live lives free from debt and poverty, and He wants us to live free from all of the things that our enemy (Satan) has put into our lives. But we have to know Him and His Word in order to do that. The Bible says in Hosea 4:6, "My people are destroyed from lack of knowledge." If you don't know and believe what the Word of God says, then how are you supposed to receive that which you know not?

I was saddened. A friend of mine was really excited about a Bible study and class that her church was putting on about healing. She was saying that they were learning a lot, and she was really enjoying all that she was learning. She then went on to say that she knew that if she expected to have any healing she had to start doing things right and eating healthier, etc. She then said that if a person eats pork it is no longer a sin, but that they will go to heaven a lot earlier than if they were not eating pork. I am not in any way saying a person shouldn't live a balanced life, including how we eat, because our bodies are temples of the Most High, but I am saying that doing things to receive a gift that has already been bought and paid for is once again not only in vain but is belittling to what Jesus did on the cross. Once again, it is using a works mentality to get something that is already ours and is free for the taking. We do not have to do anything to earn healing. We do not need to stop sinning, eating poorly, etc., because that would be working to get it, and in working it would be an obligation on God's part. But He is not paying us with healing. We can never work hard enough for healing, and we can never earn anything from God. God has given it to us free and clear, without any reservations and without any stipulations except just to have faith and believe.

Smith Wigglesworth was an amazing man of God. In the book titled *The Life of Smith Wigglesworth, A Pioneer of the Pentecostal Movement* it tells about the life and ministry of Smith Wigglesworth and about all of the great things that took place under his ministry. Smith Wigglesworth was a man of boldness. He acted out his faith in wonderful, mighty ways that stunned many.

In reading about one of the many stories of his faith it talks about how he was on a ship going to New Zealand and Australia. On the ship the entertainment officer asked Smith if he would like to be a part of the entertainment, and of course, never giving up the opportunity to share his faith, he told the entertainment officer that he would love to be a part of it and to put him down for singing. When it came time for his song he handed a copy of the song to the pianist, who, after looking over it with a look of horror, refused to accompany him. Without any thought he started to sing a song about the Lord and all that He has done for us. Some people complained, and yet others were changed.[1]

The next morning a young couple approached Smith and told him about a lady who was so ill that the ship's doctor gave little hope for her. The lady was a Christian Scientist and was one of the greatest Christian Scientist teachers. Smith agreed to see the lady and "with his usual abruptness said, 'I'm not going to speak to you about anything. Not about your sickness, or anything. I am simply going to lay hands on you and in the name of Jesus, and the moment I do, you will be healed.'"[2]

He then placed his hands on her and immediately she was healed.

> The effect on her was one of bewilderment. For three days she walked the decks greatly troubled. But Wigglesworth resisted the temptation to talk to her. He waited for the Holy Spirit to speak to her first. Feeling greatly puzzled she called for Smith to visit her once more.
>
> "What shall I do?" she asked him. "What do you mean?" he replied. "For three years I have been preaching about Christian Science all over England. We live in a great house in India, and we have another large house in London. But now my life has been changed. This is the real thing, I am a new woman." She told him that she had a new joy, but then asked: "Shall I be able to continue smoking cigarettes?" To her astonishment he said, "Yes, of course you can. Smoke as many as you can. Smoke night and day, if you can."[3]

She then asked him about playing cards and drinking wine, and his answer was always the same, he told her to do all of those things, adding, "If you can."[4]

The ship continued to sail, and by this time many

changes were taking place in this woman. Smith knew that if he had ordered her to give up these things in her life then it would be done in works, rather than that of faith through the workings of the Holy Spirit.

> On their arrival at Aden she instructed the maid to take a message to the ship's wireless officer. It was to cancel a consignment of cigarettes she had ordered before leaving London. "My life has changed. I cannot go along with all these things again," was her explanation.[5]

If we do things with a works mentality we will be like Martha, concerned and stressed about many things, because when things are demanded of us we will get overwhelmed and our hearts will not be right. But when we do things in faith we are free. When we give our lives to Christ, change is inevitable. We want to change because we love God, but if we change because it is demanded of us, that change is not done in faith but in works; that change will never last. We need to find God, fall in love with God, and when we do change will happen—and it will be real, not manufactured.

And, just like healing, we cannot work for these things Christ has freely given to us, because then it would be on our merit, ability, accomplishments, capabilities, skills, and excellence, versus a free gift from God that was paid for on the cross.

7

HOSEA AND GOMER

God's Great Love for His Unfaithful Bride

My beloved spoke and said to me, "Arise, my darling, my beautiful one, come with me. See! The winter is past; the rains are over and gone. Flowers appear on the earth; the season of singing has come, the cooing of doves is heard in our land. The fig tree forms its early fruit; the blossoming vines spread their fragrance. Arise, come, my darling; my beautiful one, come with me."

—Song of Songs 2:10–13

Have you ever felt utterly lonely? So lonely that you almost physically hurt? Have you ever hurt so badly from all that life has thrown at you that you were ready to be done? Have you felt unloved, abandoned, worthless, and rejected? Do you feel like you have the weight of the world on your back and you're crumbling under the pressure? Is nothing working out the way you thought it would or should? No matter what you do, is it ever enough?

We've all gone through times in our lives where we've felt these feelings and thought these thoughts. I still go through these times in my life, although the closer I get to God the farther I get from these lies that Satan tells us. You may feel lonely, but the truth is you are never alone.

> For he hath said, I will never leave thee, nor forsake thee.
>
> —HEBREWS 13:5, KJV

You may feel ugly and unwanted, but the truth is you are beautiful and uniquely created.

> I will praise thee; for I am fearfully and wonderfully made: marvellous are thy works.
>
> —PSALM 139:14, KJV

You may feel the weight of the world on you shoulders, but the truth is, God is willing to carry your burdens. He will never give you more than you can bear.

> For my yoke is easy, and my burden is light.
>
> —MATTHEW 11:30

You may feel weak, but the truth is, in Christ Jesus you are *strong*.

> My grace is sufficient for thee: for my strength is made perfect in weakness. Most gladly therefore will I rather glory in my infirmities, that the power of Christ may rest upon me.
>
> —2 CORINTHIANS 12:9, KJV

You may feel worthless, but the truth is, Jesus died for you because He looks at you as worth everything.

> Are not five sparrows sold for two pennies? Yet not one of them is forgotten by God. Indeed, the very hairs of your head are all numbered. Don't be afraid; you are worth more than many sparrows.
>
> —LUKE 12:6–7

God looks at you as more than enough, highly valued, wanted, and loved more than you could ever imagine. He wants to romance us and heal all of our hurts.

There are so many movies out about love. They show this kind of love that is humanly impossible, and it causes people to have this false expectation of what they want from another human. I watched a movie quite a few years ago. It was at a time in my life where I still looked to my husband to fill in the void in my heart when I should have been looking to God to do that. When you look to God to meet all of your needs, especially the emotional ones, you will truly never be the same.

So, the movie I watched was about a man and woman who fell in love, but just before they had the chance to get married and live happily ever after the man was sent off to war. The only physical contact they had was a kiss that was given right before the man left. For over three years the woman lived and waited for his return because of her great and passionate love for him, and the man fought every single day so that he could return to his beloved. He survived great obstacles just to get back to her. Before the woman's father died he had told her that he was married to her mother for a very short time, but the love they shared was enough to last a lifetime.

The man finally returned from war, they spent one

passionate night together, and then the man died. But it was enough love to last for the rest of her life.

After watching this movie I felt hurt and jealous. I couldn't believe that there could be a love like that, a love that was so passionate that a moment could last forever. I wondered why I didn't have that kind of love, and like every honest female I desperately wanted it. I wanted to be romanced and swept off my feet. I wanted my husband to love me with such passion that he'd do anything for me, that he'd think of me night and day and want me so badly.

While I was sitting there feeling depressed and thinking that I couldn't be loved with that kind of passion, I suddenly heard the Lord speak to me and say, "I love you that passionately. I'd walk the world over for you. You are My beloved. I love you, and I'd do anything for you. I died for you so that you could be with Me for all eternity. I think of you day and night and long to be with you, fellowship with you, and be one with you." God wants to have a love relationship with all of us. He wants to sweep us all off our feet and show us the passion He has for us.

My husband was ministering to a woman, and God gave my husband an incredible vision for this woman he didn't even know. He later told me about it, and I thought the vision was so incredible I wrote it down so that I wouldn't forget it. In the vision this lady was dancing on a floor that was littered with bricks that she couldn't see, and as she danced she kept falling and tripping over all of the unseen debris. Across the dance floor the Lord sat on a bench. Finally, unable to dance anymore, she cried out to the Lord. The Lord came over, picked her up off the floor, and danced with her. Even though the bricks and debris still littered the dance floor, they were able to dance through the debris without it even having the slightest effect on their perfect union. With God it didn't matter; the floor was smooth, as if the bricks and debris weren't even there. This really hit the woman, because she really liked dancing and really needed to give herself and her problems over to God. There are going to be many obstacles in life, but with God, life can still be full of peace and joy unspeakable.

There is this incredible, spontaneous song that is on a CD called *The River 5*. The song is called "A Love Like This." A man and women do a duet. The duet is supposed to be a love song between God and man. The man is crying out to God saying that he wants to get closer to God, how he reserves nothing for his own, and how God has consumed him. Some of the lyrics of the song have God saying to man:

> I've had my eye on you from the day I formed you, fashioned you within your mother's womb. I've had you in my gaze. I would never, never give you a place to go that would be out of my sight. You're my delight and I always, always want you in my gaze. There's no reason for you to hide from me, because I'm here to set you free. Free from condemnation, free from the lies of the enemy. As he comes to mock you and to taunt you, oh I am here to set you free. I am here for you. I love you...I love you with a perfect love, and I cast down all fear in you. Rest in me and draw closer. I'm jealous over you, oh so jealous over you, and I want all of you, not

> just part of you...I will give you all that you desire...We are one. Do you know what that means?...I want to invade your very being. I want to rush in; I want my voice to reverberate inside you, shaking you to the very core, with my love for you rearranging all your thoughts until they line up with my thoughts.[1]

Up until this point we've compared different people. In comparing the different people we have discovered a little about what God desires for us. He has revealed to us what He wants us to be and not to be. We've learned that God wants us to desire Him above all else, loving Him and others the way He loves us. God wants us to trust in Him and who He is, knowing that His love for us is perfect. The Lord wants us to give not only our best to Him but our all. He doesn't want us compromising and taking less then His best. And God wants us to fear Him, respect Him, and adore Him, for He is *great*!

In this chapter we are not so much going to compare two people as look at their lives. By looking at the lives of these two people we will better see the great, passionate, furious, wild, and romantic love that God has for us, His people.

Here we have a prophet and a prostitute. You are probably thinking, What could a prophet and a prostitute ever have in common? The answer is, one of the greatest love stories in the Bible. The story is that of Hosea and Gomer. On the surface it seems a little crazy—here the Lord asks a man to marry a prostitute, who continues in her adulterous ways. Where is the love and romance in that? But upon further inspection it really is an amazing story about God's unfailing love for His beautiful bride.

During the time of Hosea and Gomer, Jeroboam II was king. During his time as king there was an outpouring of money from other nations, and Israel was in a time of financial prosperity but spiritual poverty. History records that because of the idolatry there was drunkenness, human sacrifice, and shrine prostitution. When you find these kinds of vile sins, you will find a large array of other sins that keep the people far from God.

In Hosea 4:1–3, it says:

> There is no faithfulness, no love, no acknowledgment of God in the land. There is only cursing, lying and murder, stealing and adultery; they break all bounds, and bloodshed follows bloodshed. Because of this the land dries up, and all who live in it waste away; the beasts of the field, the birds in the sky and the fish in the sea are swept away.

Sin saddens God, because He sees what it does to the people, how it wreaks havoc on lives and puts them into great bondage and along with it brings judgment. Satan goes before God's throne (Job 1:1–6), and any time people sin Satan brings up that sin before God. Because God has given people free will He can't make anyone do anything that they are not willing to do. When a person sins the sin opens a door, which allows Satan to come into their lives and cause great devastation. Our world is full of pain and suffering. All of the devastation, loss, pain, and corruption in our world is caused by people's sin and the open doorway that their sin created.

God looks at His people as His wife, so idolatry is in all actuality adultery to God. To God, the people—His people, whom He loved—were committing spiritual adultery by worshiping other gods.

So, God told one of his prophets to marry a prostitute.

> When the LORD began to speak through Hosea, the LORD said to him, "Go, marry a promiscuous woman and have children with her, for like an adulterous wife this land is guilty of unfaithfulness to the LORD." So he married Gomer daughter of Diblaim, and she conceived and bore him a son. Then the LORD said to Hosea, "Call him Jezreel, because I will soon punish the house of Jehu for the massacre at Jezreel, and I will put an end to the kingdom of Israel. In that day I will break Israel's bow in the Valley of Jezreel."
>
> —HOSEA 1:2–5

The Lord had Hosea name the baby Jezreel because of its prophetic meaning to His people.

The prophet Elisha told another prophet of God to go to Gilead, where Jehu, son of Jehoshaphat, was. So the prophet went and found Jehu. As Elisha had commanded, the prophet took Jehu away from his companions, poured oil over him, and declared that he was now king over the Lord's people, Israel. Speaking through the prophet, God told Jehu to go and destroy the house of Ahab and avenge the blood of the prophets. After telling Jehu all that the Lord had for him, the prophet opened the door and ran out. Jehu went out to his fellow officers. One of the officers asked what the prophet of God had said, so Jehu told them. The men hurried and took their cloaks and spread them under Jehu, and blew the trumpet shouting, "Jehu is king!" (See 2 Kings 9.)

> So Jehu killed everyone in Jezreel who remained of the house of Ahab, as well as all his chief men, his close friends and his priests, leaving him no survivor.
>
> —2 Kings 10:11

After killing everyone in the house of Ahab, Jehu brought all of the Baal worshipers in the land together and killed them all, destroying Baal worship in Israel.

> However, he did not turn away from the sins of Jeroboam son of Nebat, which he had caused Israel to commit—the worship of the golden calves at Bethel and Dan.
>
> —2 Kings 10:29

> When the Lord began to speak through Hosea, the Lord said to him, "Go, marry a promiscuous woman and have children with her, for like an adulterous wife this land is guilty of unfaithfulness to the Lord." So he married Gomer daughter of Diblaim, and she conceived and bore him a son. Then the Lord said to Hosea, "Call him Jezreel, because I will soon punish the house of Jehu for the massacre at Jezreel, and I will put an end to the kingdom of Israel. In that day I will break Israel's bow in the Valley of Jezreel."
>
> —Hosea 1:2–5

Because of Israel's unfaithfulness to God, God was saying that judgment was coming, just like in Jezreel. The household of Ahab had sinned greatly against God, and judgment came. God also said that He would "break

Israel's bow." The bow was a symbol of victory. Because of their sin they would no longer have the victory that they once knew.

I've seen different people who once walked close to God, and then life and sin stepped in; chaos followed. The victories that they once knew were no longer. I look at those people, and my heart aches for them. They once walked in light and victory, and now they walk in darkness, all because of the choices they made and continue to make.

So, the Bible says that Gomer conceived again and gave birth to a baby girl. The Lord told Hosea that he was to call the baby girl Lo-Ruhamah, which means "not loved." Shortly after that she gave birth to a baby boy, and the Lord told Hosea to name him Lo-Ammi, which means "not my people."

All three names have prophetic significance. God told His prophet Hosea to marry a prostitute so He could show through the life of Hosea, the way He felt for His people. Hosea and Gomer were models, per se, for God and His people. God's people were turning to other gods, forgetting their first love. God tells His people that judgment is coming, and the wayward people continued wandering away from God.

And then for the big blow to faithful Hosea: Gomer has Lo-Ammi, and he then realizes that the baby isn't his. Gomer, who was once an adulterous woman, was now being unfaithful again, just as God's people were being unfaithful to Him and even raising their children not to know and love God.

But here is where the love story comes into play. What an incredible movie this story would make. You have this wonderful man who loves God. He goes and chooses this wife, who is a prostitute. He brings her out of the demeaning life of prostitution. Then Hosea shows her this great love. They have three beautiful children, and then he realizes that she is cheating on him. For many of you, you can imagine the blow that that had to have had on Hosea, that feeling of utter rejection and of feeling betrayed in one of the greatest ways a person can feel betrayed. The hurt and sadness that followed had to have been awful.

But the story doesn't end there. Many times in life, just when you think things couldn't get any worse, the bottom falls out, and that is exactly what happened to Hosea. Gomer decides to leave Hosea and continue in her unfaithful ways. The Bible says she runs after her lovers and is unable to catch them. She soon realizes that the grass truly isn't greener on the other side. Gomer then acknowledges that Hosea was the one who fed her and lavished on her silver and gold. But at this point, what can she do? She had committed the greatest offense that one could in the covenant relationship of marriage.

> The LORD said to me, "Go, show your love to your wife again, though she is loved by another man and is an adulteress. Love her as the LORD loves the Israelites, though they turn to other gods and love the sacred raisin cakes." So I bought her for fifteen shekels of silver and about a homer and a lethek of barley. Then I told her, "You are to live with me many days; you must not be a prostitute or be intimate with any man, and I will behave the same way toward you."
>
> —HOSEA 3:1–3

So Hosea goes and buys back his wife, forgiving her and showing her an unconditional love. This is how God is with us. He bought us with the price of His life. His love is so great, and we are so unfaithful, sinful, and unworthy of the love that He has for us; yet He is always faithful, lavishing riches and greatness upon us, even when we turn our backs on Him. God calls us worthy. He calls us His beloved, His beautiful bride! No matter what our offense is, God's forgiveness is greater.

Even after the Israelite's idolatry, the Lord says:

> Therefore I am now going to allure her; I will lead her into the wilderness and speak tenderly to her. There I will give her back her vineyards, and will make the Valley of Achor a door of hope. There she will respond as in the days of her youth, as in the day she came up out of Egypt. "In that day," declares the Lord, "you will call me 'my husband'; you will no longer call me 'my master.' I will remove the names of the Baals from her lips; no longer will their names be invoked. In that day I will make a covenant for them with the beasts of the field, the birds in the sky and the creatures that move along the ground. Bow and sword and battle I will abolish from the land, so that all may lie down in safety. I will betroth you to me forever; I will betroth you in righteousness and justice, in love and compassion. I will betroth you in faithfulness, and you will acknowledge the Lord.... I will plant her for myself in the land; I will show my love to the one I called 'Not my loved one.' I will say to those called 'Not my people,' 'You are my people'; and they will say, 'You are my God.'"
>
> —Hosea 2:14–20, 23

Doesn't every human want to be loved like that, loved unconditionally? No matter what you've done—or continue to do—you are forgiven, and it's all forgotten. And while you are surrounded by your mistakes, and your life is full of hopelessness and heartache, your beloved calls to you and allures you, powerfully attracting you out of the darkness and into the light. Because you are hurt and you've been kicked around and beaten up in life, your beloved gently guides you and softly, tenderly speaks life to you. Your beloved then turns your troubles into hope.

Because of the love you are shown, you sing like in the days of your youth, in days when troubles seemed to evade you and hope seemed to float on the clouds. When all those mistakes you've made will be removed from your very lips, and you will feel safe like never before, for your beloved will be there to protect and guide you. And then the best part: your beloved wants to marry you. But unlike the marriages you've encountered before, the marriages that are full of more heartache and pain, this is a marriage that will last forever, a marriage made up of true love and compassion. Your beloved will romance you and lavish on you blessings beyond your wildest dreams.

Do you think that this kind of love is only for fairy tales? It's not. This is the kind of love that God Almighty has for each and every one of us. You just need to cry out to Him, and He will answer you. He has put in each one of us a hole that needs to be filled. But instead of letting Him fill that void with His love, we tend to fill it with the things of the world. Things like sex outside of marriage, drugs, alcohol, the love of money, power, and every other sin that eats away at our very being, striping from us any dignity that we may have left.

As for the Israelites, they no longer ran and hid from the Lord. They finally repented, just as Gomer did, and God in His great mercy forgave His people, the Israelites. Then God blessed them. This truly is an incredible love story full of mercy and forgiveness. It's not only a great show of God's great love for us but also a guide for us to live by in our own lives. Who are we not to forgive when we have been forgiven so many times before?

Heavenly Father,

Thank You for the people reading this book. I pray that they will all walk away from this book desiring You more, that they will be set ablaze by Your Holy Fire, and that their lives will never be the same. May they desire to seek You with all of their heart. I pray that they will fall in love with You in a new way and that they may come to know the great and mighty love that You have for them, a love that changes hearts, a love that liberates, and a love that changes eternities.

Please, Lord, bless them. Let them want to run the race in order to obtain the prize! Help them to live a life worthy of the calling which they have received. May they live a life without compromise, a life where they trust You without reservation, with all of their hearts, and may they give You their best. Let them be men and women after Your own heart, and let them get to the secret place of the Most High!

Lord, I pray that these wonderful men and women may have a heart after You, Oh God. In Jesus' holy and precious name, amen!

NOTES

Chapter 1:
Jacob vs. Esau

1. Darren Wilson, as interviewed by Sid Roth, *Sid Roth's It's Supernatural*, May 7, 2010.

2. Steve Thompson, *You May All Prophesy! Practical Guidelines for Prophetic Ministry* (Fort Mill, SC: MorningStar Publications, 2000), 21.

3. Ibid., 22.

Chapter 2:
David vs. Saul

1. Connie Grigsby and Nancy Cobb, *Is There a Moose in Your Marriage: Removing the Roadblocks Through the Power of God* [renamed *The Politically Incorrect Wife: God's Plan for Marriage Still Works Today*] (Colorado Springs, CO: Multnomah Books, 2000).

Chapter 3:
Abel vs. Cain

1. Corrie ten Boom, "Love Your Enemy," *Chicken Soup for the Christian Soul*, Jack Canfield, Mark Victor Hansen, Patty Aubery, and Nancy Mitchell, eds. (Deerfield Beach, FL: HCI Books, 1997), 2–5.

2. Ibid.

3. Corrie ten Boom, with John and Elizabeth Sherrill, *The Hiding Place* (New York: Bantam Books, 1984).

4. Corrie ten Boom, "Love Your Enemy," *Chicken Soup for the Christian Soul.*

Chapter 4:
Elijah vs. Ahab

1. Wilford Reidt, *John G. Lake: A Man Without Compromise* (Tulsa, OK: Harrison House, 1989), taken from the back cover of the book.

2. Ibid., 70, 133.

3. Ibid., 78.

4. Ibid., 81–83.

5. Ibid.

6. Ibid., taken from the back cover of the book.

Chapter 5:
Joshua and Caleb vs. the Ten

1. John Bevere, *The Fear of the Lord* (Lake Mary, FL: Charisma House, 2006), 7–14.

2. Ibid.

3. Ibid.

4. Ibid.

5. Ibid.

6. Ibid.

7. Ibid.

8. Ibid.

Chapter 6:
Mary vs. Martha

1. Jack Hywel-Davies, *The Life of Smith Wigglesworth, A Pioneer of the Pentecostal Movement* (London: Hodder and Stoughton Limited, 1987), 118–122.

2. Ibid.

3. Ibid.

4. Ibid.

5. Ibid.

Chapter 7: Hosea and Gomer

1. "A Love Like This" Spontaneous Song. Performed by Robert Stearns on live worship CD River 5 *Dance with Me,* www.eagleswings.tood (http://www.eagleswings.tood).

ABOUT THE AUTHOR

FIRST OFF, I am a daughter of the Most High. I love the Lord God with all of my heart and want to honor Him with my life. I am a wife to a wonderful, godly man who I love very much, and I am a mother to seven wonderful, beautiful children. I believe that being a wife and mother is my first and most important calling, and I try very hard to be faithful to it. I am a stay-at-home mom, I do the secretarial and bookkeeping work for my husband's home-inspection business, and my husband and I also homeschool our oldest three children. I spent over a year and a half writing this book during every nap time and at nights when they were asleep, because I had very little time when they were awake to write. I realized that I really enjoy writing when it is not coming from me but from God. Writing this book has definitely stretched me and made me want to walk a better walk, live a life of love, and know God even more. For all of that, I praise Him!

CONTACT THE AUTHOR

To leave an e-mail, please visit our website:

www.heartaftergodministries.net